GOLD
BEACH

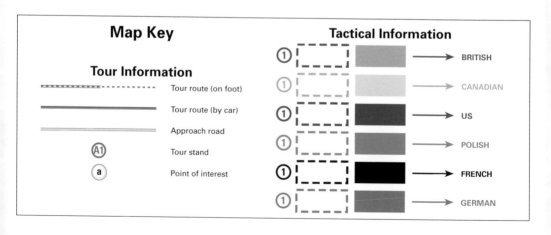

Map Key

Tour Information

···················-----------	Tour route (on foot)
————————	Tour route (by car)
————————	Approach road
(A1)	Tour stand
(a)	Point of interest

Tactical Information

(1)	▢	⬛ ⟶ BRITISH
(1)	▢	⬛ ⟶ CANADIAN
(1)	▢	⬛ ⟶ US
(1)	▢	⬛ ⟶ POLISH
(1)	▢	⬛ ⟶ FRENCH
(1)	▢	⬛ ⟶ GERMAN

PART ONE

INTRODUCTION

BATTLE ZONE NORMANDY

The Battle of Normandy was one of the greatest military clashes of all time. From late 1943, when the Allies appointed their senior commanders and began the air operations that were such a vital preliminary to the invasion, until the end of August 1944, it pitted against one another several of the most powerful nations on earth, as well as some of their most brilliant minds. When it was won, it changed the world forever. The price was high, but for anybody who values the principles of freedom and democracy, it is difficult to conclude that it was one not worth paying.

I first visited Lower Normandy in 1994, a year after I joined the War Studies Department at the Royal Military Academy Sandhurst (RMAS). With the 50th anniversary of D-Day looming, it was decided that the British Army would be represented at several major ceremonies by one of the RMAS's officer cadet companies. It was also suggested that the cadets should visit some of the battlefields, not least to bring home to them the significance of why they were there. Thus, at the start of June 1994, I found myself as one of a small team of military and civilian directing staff flying with the cadets in a draughty and noisy Hercules transport to visit the beaches and fields of Calvados, in my case for the first time.

I was hooked. Having met some of the veterans and seen the ground over which they fought – and where many of their friends died – I was determined to go back. Fortunately, the Army encourages battlefield study as part of its soldiers' education, and on numerous occasions since 1994 I have been privileged to return to Normandy, often to visit new sites. In the process I have learned a vast amount, both from my colleagues (several of whom were contributors to the original Battle Zone Normandy series) and from my enthusiastic and sometimes tri-service audiences, whose professional insights and penetrating questions have frequently made me re-examine my own assumptions and prejudices. Perhaps inevitably, especially when standing in one of Normandy's beautifully-maintained Commonwealth War Graves Commission cemeteries, I have also found myself deeply moved by the critical events that took place there in the summer of 1944.

The original 'Battle Zone Normandy' series was conceived by Jonathan Falconer, Commissioning Editor at Sutton Publishing, in 2001. Why not, he suggested, bring together recent academic research – some of which challenges the general perception of what happened on and after 6 June 1944 – with a perspective based on familiarity with the ground itself? We agreed that the opportunity existed for a series that would set out to combine detailed and accurate narratives, based mostly on primary sources, with illustrated guides to the ground itself, which could be used either in the field (sometimes quite literally), or by the armchair explorer. The book in your hands is the product of that agreement.

The 'Battle Zone Normandy' series consisted of 14 volumes, covering most of the major and many of the minor engagements that went together to create the Battle of Normandy. The first six books deal with the airborne and amphibious landings on 6 June 1944, and with the struggle to create the firm lodgement that was the prerequisite for eventual Allied victory. Five further volumes cover some of the critical battles that followed, as the Allies' plans unravelled and they were forced to improvise a battle very different from that originally intended. Finally, the last three titles in the series examine the fruits of the bitter attritional struggle of June and July 1944, as the Allies irrupted through the German lines or drove them back in fierce fighting. The series ends, logically enough, with the devastation of the German armed forces in the 'Falaise Pocket' in late August.

Whether you use these books while visiting Normandy, or to experience the battlefields vicariously, we hope you will find them as interesting to read as we did to research and write. Far from the inevitable victory that is sometimes represented, D-Day and the ensuing battles were full of hazards and unpredictability. Contrary to the view often expressed, had the invasion failed, it is far from certain that a second attempt could have been mounted. Remember this, and the significance of the contents of this book, not least for your life today, will be the more obvious.

Dr Simon Trew,
Royal Military Academy Sandhurst,
December 2003

R. Rhine

GERMANY

LUX

NETHERLANDS

BELGIUM

Brussels

FRANCE

R. Seine

R. Loire

Amiens

La Roche Guyon

Paris

Rouen

Le Mans

Le Havre

Caen

St. Lô

Rennes

Cherbourg

Brest

GREAT BRITAIN

London

Newhaven

Portsmouth

Southampton

Poole

Weymouth

Dartmouth

Plymouth

ENGLISH CHANNEL

21st Army Group

XXXX
FIFTEENTH
1 SS(-)

165
712
19 GAF
48
18 GAF
182
331(-)
326
A
47
49
344
85
348
245
B
17 GAF
84
346
711
12 SS
116
LEHR
2

FIFTEENTH
XXXX
SEVENTH

17 SS(-)

716
21
352
C
91
709
243
77
5 PARA(-)
319
266
3 PARA
353
343
265
275(-)
D
158

B
XXXXX
G

German Order of Battle 6 June 1944

Town	●
Int. boundary	–·–·–
–XXXX–	Army boundary
–XXXXX–	Army Group boundary
	Static or reserve division ▢
	Attack infantry division ☒
	Panzergrenadier division ☒
	Panzer division ▢
	Division forming or rehabilitating (-)

Ⓐ Pas de Calais
Ⓑ Upper Normandy
Ⓒ Lower Normandy
Ⓓ Brittany

Kilometres
0   50   100

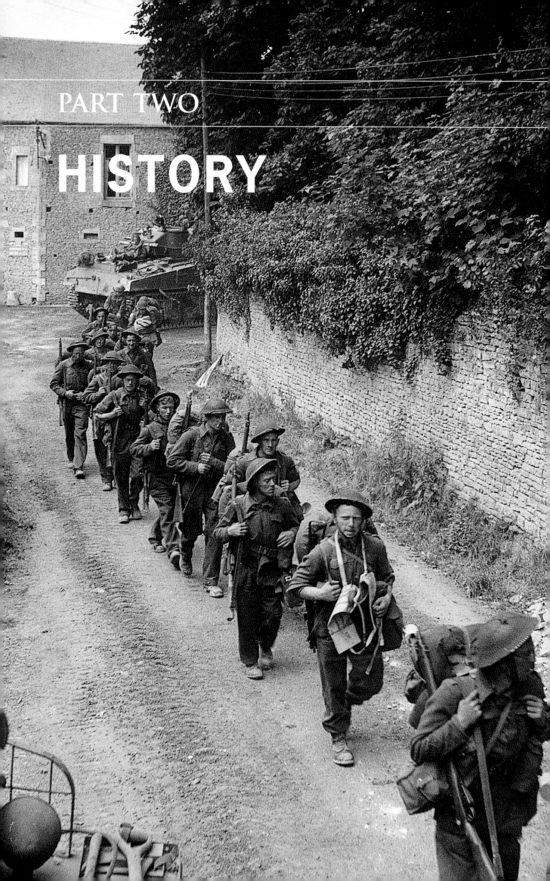

PART TWO

HISTORY

CHAPTER 1

THE DEFENDERS

Page 11: British personnel join the advance inland, 6 June 1944. (IWM B5250)

Below: A 1930s image of the beach at Ver-sur-Mer. Most of the villas shown were demolished by the Germans to clear fields of fire, or destroyed in the fighting on D-Day. The sea wall still existed in 1944 and was used as cover by men of 5th East Yorks before they stormed the la Rivière strongpoint. (Dupont collection)

In early 1944 Ver-sur-Mer was a typically pretty Norman seaside village of some 700 people. Situated roughly 20 kilometres (km) north-west of Caen, the principal urban centre of the Calvados *département* in Lower Normandy, it possessed an attractive château and an impressive 11th-century church tower. As elsewhere along the Calvados coast, it also benefited from a fine, gently shelving beach, the sands of which stretched at low tide almost a thousand metres beyond the high water mark. This had made Ver-sur-Mer popular with tourists long before the war, and by the early 1900s dozens of holiday villas – many of them large and imposing – had been built just behind the shore. On some maps these houses appeared as a discrete settlement called la Rivière. To the locals, however, the area was usually known simply as *la Plage* (the beach).

Like many French villages titled '*sur-mer*' (literally 'on sea'), the centre of Ver-sur-Mer actually lies slightly inland, in a slight depression on the northern slopes of a low

(40–60 metres) ridge. This feature runs broadly parallel with the coast and offers excellent visibility in both directions. From just north-west of Ver, for example, it is possible to observe the entire shoreline – and the marshes behind it – as far as Asnelles, at the mouth of a broad valley 4 km distant, and beyond it to the cliffs near Arromanches-les-Bains. Looking east, the ridge provides views towards the minor port of Courseulles-sur-Mer. Because of its elevated position, Ver also provided the location for a lighthouse, built on a small knoll called Mont Fleury. This warned sailors of the presence of offshore reefs between Asnelles and Courseulles, and acted as a navigation beacon for coastal traffic.

In addition to its native inhabitants, by the spring of 1944 Ver had become home to hundreds of foreigners. Many were Germans or *Volksdeutsche* (ethnic Germans from outside pre-war Germany), but there were also several hundred Russians. A few were civilians, but most were members of the *Wehrmacht* (Nazi Germany's armed forces), among them middle-aged fortress engineers and gunners from an Army coastal artillery battery. The majority, however, came from 716th Infantry Division and its attached units. Conspicuous among the latter were three companies of former Red Army prisoners of war, under the command of German officers. These were part of 441st *Ost* ('East') Battalion, the headquarters of which was at Marefontaine farm on Ver's southern outskirts. Other important sub-units of the 716th Division in the immediate area included 7th Company, 736th Grenadier Regiment, in la Rivière, and 6th Battery, 1716th Artillery Regiment, located in concrete gun emplacements 500 metres east of Marefontaine farm.

Although there had been Germans in Calvados ever since June 1940, the presence of so many troops in Ver-sur-Mer was a relatively recent phenomenon. Until late 1943 Lower Normandy had been regarded as an unlikely area for an Allied invasion. With the exception of the port facilities at Cherbourg, at the northern end of the Cotentin peninsula, little serious work had been done to make the coastline defensible. The *Wehrmacht* garrison was also generally

The view from
the old quarry
north-west of
Ver-sur-Mer,
looking west. The
marshes behind
the shoreline and
the cliffs beyond
Arromanches are
clearly visible. In
1944 the quarry,
which is about
40 metres above
sea level, formed
part of the
German defences
overlooking Gold
Beach. (Author)

of low calibre. This was especially true of 716th Infantry Division, which arrived in March 1942 with only 6,000 men (a full strength combat division had 15,000), mainly drawn from personnel deemed unsuitable for service in the east. The division was ordered to protect the entire coastline from Carentan, near the mouth of the River Douve on the Cotentin, all the way to Franceville-Plage, east of the River Orne. Given that this was around 90 km, the division was very thinly spread. Unsurprisingly, when told by the *Kriegsmarine* (German Navy) that the offshore reefs around Ver-sur-Mer precluded a landing here, the division's commander made little effort to fortify the village or to occupy it strongly.

In autumn 1943, however, significant changes began to make themselves felt. The military strength and successes of the British and Americans meant that the Germans were now forced to acknowledge the likelihood of an invasion the following year. If the *Westheer* (the generic title for the German Army in the west) met a major attack in its current condition, the Third Reich's defeat was almost inevitable. Recognising this, on 3 November 1943 Hitler issued Führer Directive 51, which listed a range of measures designed to improve the *Wehrmacht*'s fighting power in France, Belgium, the Netherlands and Denmark. Two days later *Generalfeldmarschall* (Field Marshal) Erwin Rommel – one of Germany's finest tacticians – was appointed by Hitler to inspect the coastal defences facing the United Kingdom (the so-called 'Atlantic Wall'), and to make plans for their improvement.

The effects of Directive 51 were soon felt. Thanks to a manpower drive, hundreds of thousands of reinforcements were sent to the *Westheer*. Many were new recruits, but there were also large numbers of tough ideologically-indoctrinated veterans from the east (known as *Ostkämpfer* – 'east fighters'). They brought valuable combat experience to the western divisions, few of whose soldiers had ever fired a shot in anger. A dozen new infantry divisions were raised and existing formations were reinforced. In addition, large quantities of the most modern types of tanks, guns and other equipment poured west, either for use in the coastal defences or by the mobile reserves that were being created inland.

The *Westheer* had a number of armies, and all of them benefited from these measures. The Fifteenth Army, which was protecting the Pas de Calais and Upper Normandy (the area immediately north and south of the River Seine), was the first to be strengthened. This was because of the proximity of this region to southern England, which made it the obvious place for an invasion. However Seventh Army, whose LXXXIV Corps defended Lower Normandy, also received reinforcement. 716th Infantry Division was transformed. The division grew considerably, from only 6,000 men in June 1943 to over 9,000 by December.

Field Marshal Rommel (*third left, with baton*) inspects the Atlantic Wall defences. On the far left is GenLt Hans Speidel, Rommel's chief of staff from 15 April 1944. (*Bundesarchiv 298/1758/19*)

Ostkämpfer took command of most of the infantry companies. Older personnel were transferred and replaced by younger men; the average age in the 716th fell from 36 to less than 30 years. The division's artillery and anti-tank capability was expanded, and its mobility improved a little. Finally, three *Osttruppen* ('eastern soldiers') battalions composed of former Soviet prisoners – many of whom had 'volunteered' to join the *Wehrmacht* only to escape their captors' murderous brutality – were added to the division's order of battle. One of these was 441st *Ost* Battalion, which was attached to 716th Infantry Division on 19 March 1944.

In another significant development, at the end of 1943 a new unit began forming around the town of St-Lô, 55 km west of Caen. This was 352nd Infantry Division, commanded by *Generalleutnant* (GenLt) Dietrich Kraiss (written as Kraiß in German), a veteran of the Eastern Front. The 352nd was intended to be a fully mobile field infantry division, capable of offensive as well as defensive tasks. It therefore absorbed numerous cadres from experienced formations, as well as thousands of 18-year-old recruits. Although it took some time for it all to arrive, the division was supplied with impressive quantities of modern equipment including 10 armoured assault guns (*Sturmgeschütze*), 14 self-propelled anti-tank guns and 48 howitzers. Together with its machine guns, mortars and other weapons, these gave 352nd Division considerable firepower.

In January 1944 Hitler appointed Rommel to command the Seventh and Fifteenth armies, which defended the coastline from the mouth of the Loire to the Netherlands. Rommel's headquarters, known as Army Group B (*Heeresgruppe B*), was eventually established at la Roche-Guyon, north-west of Paris. This placed it near the HQ of Field Marshal Gerd von Rundstedt, who was *Oberbefehlshaber West* (OB West or Commander-in-Chief West) and Rommel's nominal superior. Owing to Rommel's personal access to Hitler, Rundstedt had little control over the deployment of the Seventh and Fifteenth armies.

However, he did have considerable influence over the use of the *Westheer*'s reserves, notably its panzer (armoured) divisions. This fact was to have profound consequences for the Battle of Normandy.

Rommel's primary concern lay in the area from Upper Normandy to the Pas de Calais where, like many of his colleagues, he believed an assault was most probable. However, although he accepted the *Kriegsmarine*'s view that the submerged reefs off Calvados made a full-scale invasion there unlikely, Rommel was not oblivious to potential risks in Seventh Army's sector. Hitler himself also insisted that an invasion there was possible, and for any German general to ignore the *Führer*'s opinion was foolish. At the end of January 1944 Rommel made the first of several visits to the sector held by LXXXIV Corps, to inspect its defences and to try to ensure that his ideas about how to oppose an invasion were implemented there as elsewhere.

Rommel's approach to coast defence reflected his background. Unlike most of his colleagues Rommel's command experience had been gained fighting the western Allies. He was keenly aware of the strength and importance of the Allies' air and naval power. Although he hoped that the *Kriegsmarine* and *Luftwaffe* (German Air Force) might disrupt an attack, he recognised the weakness of both. By June 1944 the *Luftwaffe* could muster just 570 serviceable aircraft in the west (only 115 of them single-engined fighters), while the *Kriegsmarine*'s contribution was a few torpedo boats and destroyers and a larger number of coastal artillery batteries. Despite plans to reinforce the

Obstacles on the beach at Asnelles (le Hamel), photographed by an Allied aircraft shortly before the invasion. In the foreground are a number of vertical posts, plus a single steel 'Belgian gate' (also known as Element C). Ramps and clusters of 'Czech hedgehogs' can also be seen. *(Tim Saunders)*

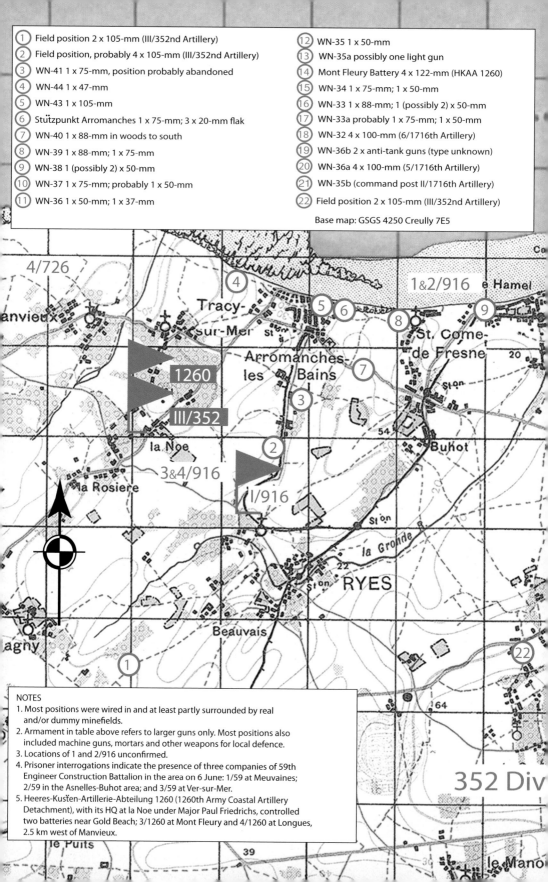

1. Field position 2 x 105-mm (III/352nd Artillery)
2. Field position, probably 4 x 105-mm (III/352nd Artillery)
3. WN-41 1 x 75-mm, position probably abandoned
4. WN-44 1 x 47-mm
5. WN-43 1 x 105-mm
6. Stützpunkt Arromanches 1 x 75-mm; 3 x 20-mm flak
7. WN-40 1 x 88-mm in woods to south
8. WN-39 1 x 88-mm; 1 x 75-mm
9. WN-38 1 (possibly 2) x 50-mm
10. WN-37 1 x 75-mm; probably 1 x 50-mm
11. WN-36 1 x 50-mm; 1 x 37-mm
12. WN-35 1 x 50-mm
13. WN-35a possibly one light gun
14. Mont Fleury Battery 4 x 122-mm (HKAA 1260)
15. WN-34 1 x 75-mm; 1 x 50-mm
16. WN-33 1 x 88-mm; 1 (possibly 2) x 50-mm
17. WN-33a probably 1 x 75-mm; 1 x 50-mm
18. WN-32 4 x 100-mm (6/1716th Artillery)
19. WN-36b 2 x anti-tank guns (type unknown)
20. WN-36a 4 x 100-mm (5/1716th Artillery)
21. WN-35b (command post II/1716th Artillery)
22. Field position 2 x 105-mm (III/352nd Artillery)

Base map: GSGS 4250 Creully 7E5

NOTES
1. Most positions were wired in and at least partly surrounded by real and/or dummy minefields.
2. Armament in table above refers to larger guns only. Most positions also included machine guns, mortars and other weapons for local defence.
3. Locations of 1 and 2/916 unconfirmed.
4. Prisoner interrogations indicate the presence of three companies of 59th Engineer Construction Battalion in the area on 6 June: 1/59 at Meuvaines; 2/59 in the Asnelles-Buhot area; and 3/59 at Ver-sur-Mer.
5. Heeres-Küsten-Artillerie-Abteilung 1260 (1260th Army Coastal Artillery Detachment), with its HQ at la Noe under Major Paul Friedrichs, controlled two batteries near Gold Beach; 3/1260 at Mont Fleury and 4/1260 at Longues, 2.5 km west of Manvieux.

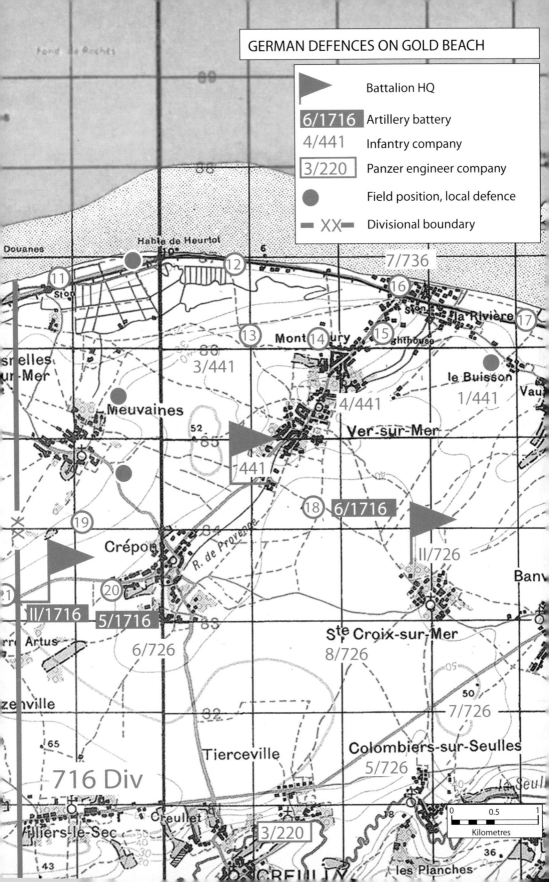

GERMAN DEFENCES ON GOLD BEACH

▶	Battalion HQ
6/1716	Artillery battery
4/441	Infantry company
3/220	Panzer engineer company
⬤	Field position, local defence
▬ XX ▬	Divisional boundary

716 Div

Luftwaffe and to send U-boats to attack Allied shipping once the invasion started, Rommel was justifiably pessimistic about the prospects of both.

The German Army, therefore, would bear the weight of the forthcoming battle. Yet to Rommel the preferred German method of land warfare – using mobile forces to encircle the enemy in a battle of annihilation – appeared impracticable. He believed that, if the *Westheer* allowed the Allied forces to get ashore, and then waited for them to advance in strength before counter-attacking, the results would be disastrous. In particular, Allied air superiority would render German mobile reserves powerless. In the coastal hinterland any large-scale movement would risk being smashed by naval gunfire. Rommel concluded that the only way to defeat an invasion was by concentrated firepower in the immediate vicinity of the coastline. This meant pushing every available asset as close to the sea as possible, digging in and forming an impenetrable barrier before the attackers arrived. Conscious that he could not be strong everywhere, Rommel also ordered the maximum use of minefields and other static barriers. Finally, he instructed that anti-landing obstacles be strewn across the beaches, and measures taken to deal with attack by airborne forces, especially by erecting thousands of wooden poles in any area where the enemy might try to land gliders.

In early 1944 352nd Infantry Division was ordered to leave its concentration area around St-Lô, and move closer to the sea. This was because Rommel believed that LXXXIV Corps was devoting too much effort to creating reserves, at the expense of its primary mission of securing the coast. Consequently, although the 352nd was still only half-trained, on 15 March it took command of Coast Defence Sector 'Bayeux', which extended from Carentan in the west to Asnelles in the east. The 716th Infantry Division retained responsibility for Coast Defence Sector 'Caen'. This continued for about 35 km from the outskirts of Asnelles to the existing divisional boundary (which was also the eastern boundary of LXXXIV Corps and Seventh Army) on the right bank of the Orne.

Logically, 352nd Division's arrival should have displaced 716th Infantry Division east, resulting in the strengthening of the Caen Defence Sector. However, substantial elements of the 716th stayed where they were, being placed under Kraiss' command. They included the headquarters and three of the four infantry battalions of 726th Grenadier Regiment, and one of the division's three artillery battalions. Most of these remained in their previous positions on or near the coast, while troops from the 352nd reinforced them or took up positions a little inland. One result was that 726th Grenadier Regiment, commanded by *Oberst* (Colonel) Walter Korfes, took charge of the most easterly of Kraiss' three coastal sub-sectors. This extended for some 15 km, most of which was cliffs, but which also included Port-en-Bessin in the west and Asnelles in the east. The regimental staff was 6 km inland, in a château at Sully. In addition to the 1st Battalion of his own 726th Regiment (I/GR 726), Korfes was given tactical control of two of the 352nd's sub-units. These were 1st Battalion, 916th Grenadier Regiment (I/GR 916) and 3rd Battalion, 352nd Artillery Regiment (III/AR 352), both of which deployed in the eastern part of Korfes' zone, near Arromanches.

Once his division was in place, Kraiss strove to improve the coastal defences. Despite shortages of labour and materials, his men built blockhouses and bunkers, dug trenches and anti-tank ditches, and laid barbed wire and minefields. In Colonel Korfes' sector the upper half of the beach at Asnelles was covered with concrete, steel and wooden obstacles. Many of these had mines and artillery shells attached, to destroy or damage landing craft before they could disembark their cargoes. Because the *Wehrmacht* expected the invasion at high tide (which would allow the attackers to shelter in their vessels to within a few metres of the foremost defence positions), obstacles were not laid near – or beyond – the low water mark. This was also true on the beaches near Ver-sur-Mer, in 716th Division's sector. Here, since the rocks off la Rivière posed additional problems for an attacker at low tide, little effort was made to extend the obstacle belt. Unfortunately for the Germans, from Ver

This photograph of Asnelles shows the view looking west from the junction of the Boulevard de la Mer and the path to WN-38. Several pre-war villas survive in this area, among them the rather impressive structure to the left. *(Author)*

westwards there was a 5-km gap in the reefs. Although greater efforts were made to obstruct this area, by June 1944 the work was still incomplete.

Behind the shoreline, in Normandy and elsewhere, the defences were laid out according to principles of mutual support, and comprised three main types of position. The first was called the *Stützpunkt* (strongpoint), which in theory was held by around 100 men armed with numerous heavy weapons. The only confirmed example in the area of Asnelles and Ver-sur-Mer was at a radar station on the cliffs near Arromanches, and this appears to have been lightly defended. Much more common were the *Widerstandsnester* (WN), or resistance nests. In the coastal zone these held

One of the Longues Battery casemates, with the 150-mm gun still in place. The battery was part of *Heeres-Küsten-Artillerie-Abteilung 1260* (Army Coastal Artillery Detachment 1260), which also controlled the Mont Fleury battery. *(Author)*

The Mont Fleury Battery was considerably less developed than the position at Longues. This casemate existed only as a breeze block shell; the concrete had not been poured between the inner and outer walls, and the building had no roof. On D-Day the 122-mm gun that should have been here was 200 metres away, in an open field position without effective protection against Allied fire. *(Author)*

up to 50 men apiece, armed with at least one anti-tank gun and a few machine guns and mortars, usually under cover. Several also included artillery observers, to call down indirect fire from guns and mortars located inland. There were seven such positions between Ver and the western part of Asnelles, most of them adjacent to the beach. Two more *Widerstandsnester* were on the slopes overlooking Asnelles from the west, and another pair at Arromanches. Others were under construction. Finally, there were two unfinished coastal artillery batteries, which were supposed to engage the Allies while they was still at sea. Of these, the closer to completion was at Longues, 5 km west of Arromanches. This was equipped with four 150-mm naval guns, each in

The dominating positions selected for the German defences are illustrated by this view from WN-40, looking east across the valley of la Gronde Ruisseau; le Carrefour is in the foreground. The boundary between 352nd and 716th Divisions ran from left to right along the far side of the valley. *(Author)*

its own concrete bunker. These guns had a range of almost 20 km, and were manned mainly by naval personnel. Much further from completion was the Mont Fleury battery on the ridge at Ver-sur-Mer. Only one of its four 122-mm guns was under concrete on 6 June 1944.

Rommel's plan prescribed maximum firepower on the coast itself, achieved by cutting tactical reserves (and mobility) to a bare minimum. However, he could not guarantee that his directives were always followed to the letter, and in Calvados his subordinates from corps level downwards appear to have been reluctant to rely on an entirely linear defence. Despite their efforts, they were painfully aware of the shallow and incomplete nature of their positions, which seemed to make an enemy penetration inevitable. They also disliked abandoning their own doctrine, which emphasised immediate counter-attacks by local reserves, not least because their Eastern Front experiences appeared to confirm its utility. Consequently they went to great lengths to maintain forces behind the coastline. The irony, of course, was that by depriving the forward defences of manpower and weapons, they increased the chances of the very breakthrough that concerned them so much.

By June 1944, LXXXIV Corps had reserves deployed throughout Lower Normandy. Although they were not as strong as the Germans wanted, some of them were well placed to support the defenders of Asnelles and Ver-sur-Mer. Closest to the coast were elements of I/GR 916, the battalion headquarters of which was at Ryes, 2.5 km south of Arromanches. At least one of its three rifle companies (140 men) and all 12 of the battalion's 81-mm mortars were nearby. Slightly deeper inland, near Crépon (4 km south-west of la Rivière) was the 2nd Battalion of 726th Grenadier Regiment (II/GR 726), detached from Korfes' command. It was the 716th Division's main reserve. Three companies of 88-mm anti-tank guns, from 21st Panzer Division, were deployed several kilometres further south, on both sides of the Bayeux–Caen highway. (This lateral route was critical to German attempts to redeploy units after the invasion began.) Finally, south and east of Bayeux was *Kampfgruppe* (Battle Group) *Meyer*. This comprised 352nd Division's 915th Grenadier Regiment (two infantry battalions, plus infantry gun and anti-tank companies) and 352nd Fusilier Battalion (*Füsilier-Bataillon 352* – the divisional reconnaissance unit), and represented LXXXIV Corps' most important tactical reserve in Calvados. As such, it could be used almost anywhere along a 100-km front. However, reflecting concerns that 21st Panzer Division, deployed on the right of Seventh Army's sector, might be removed by Army Group B to another area in the event of an invasion, Battle Group *Meyer* paid special attention to preparing a counter-attack to the north-east, in the direction of Crépon and Ver-sur-Mer.

Had Rommel commanded the *Westheer*, all its mobile reserves would have been placed near the coast, ready to deliver concentrated counter-blows while the Allies were trying to get ashore. However, in 1944 Gerd von Rundstedt was OB West and, together with several other senior officers, he held different views. He believed that to tie the panzer divisions to coastal defence was to waste their greatest strength – their mobility – and to risk their isolation and piecemeal destruction. He wanted the armour to remain inland, positioned in a manner that would allow it to be concentrated for a decisive counter-attack once the main enemy effort was identified. Although he acknowledged the critical importance of forward defence as a means of buying time, Rundstedt thought it impossible that the Atlantic Wall could withstand a major assault. The only way to defeat the Allies would be by rapid manoeuvre aimed at their encirclement and annihilation some distance inland.

Numerous attempts were made during early 1944 to resolve the debate about the use of the *Westheer*'s reserves. However, when Hitler made his final decision in May, the outcome represented an unsatisfactory compromise. Rather than commit the German armour to one purpose under a single commander, the ten available divisions (only four of them fully operational) were split between different headquarters. Rommel's Army Group B was given control

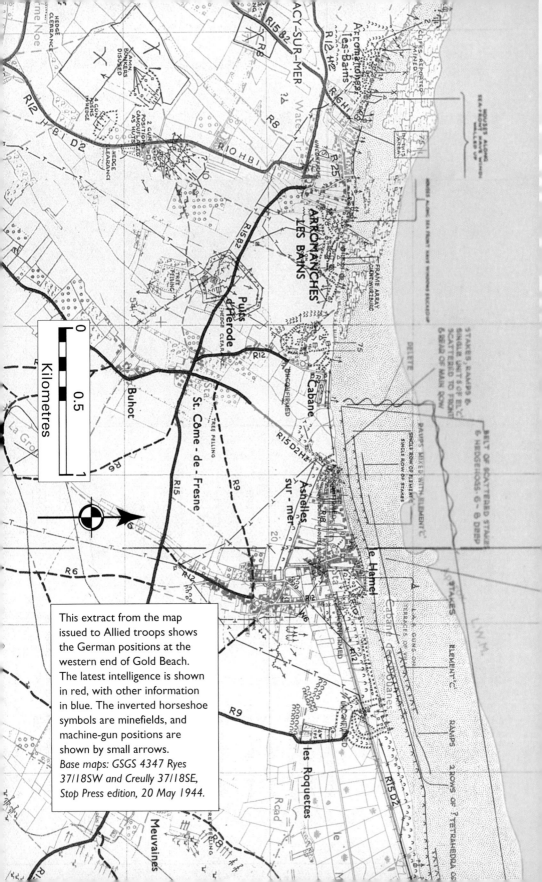

This extract from the map issued to Allied troops shows the German positions at the western end of Gold Beach. The latest intelligence is shown in red, with other information in blue. The inverted horseshoe symbols are minefields, and machine-gun positions are shown by small arrows.
Base maps: GSGS 4347 Ryes 37/18SW and Creully 37/18SE, Stop Press edition, 20 May 1944.

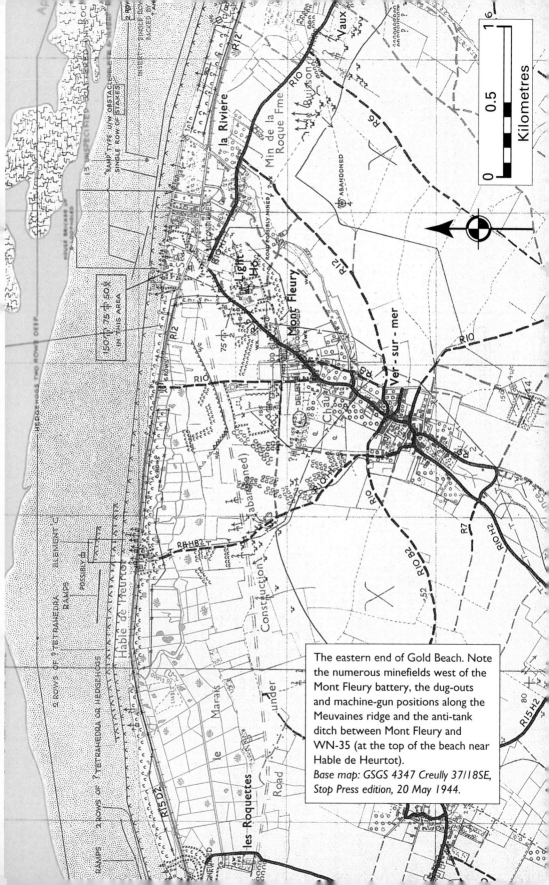

The eastern end of Gold Beach. Note the numerous minefields west of the Mont Fleury battery, the dug-outs and machine-gun positions along the Meuvaines ridge and the anti-tank ditch between Mont Fleury and WN-35 (at the top of the beach near Hable de Heurtot).
Base map: GSGS 4347 Creully 37/18SE, Stop Press edition, 20 May 1944.

In February 1944 the Allies began a massive programme of aerial bombardment, to smash German lines of communication, and restrict the arrival of reinforcements and supplies in Normandy after the invasion began. This photograph shows the railway yards and road bridge over the River Loire at Saumur following an RAF raid on the night of 1 June. *(IWM CL79)*

over just three divisions, only one of which – 21st Panzer – was deployed in Lower Normandy. Army Group G, defending southern France, received three. Finally, I SS Panzer Corps, with four divisions, was placed under the direct control of the *Oberkommando der Wehrmacht* (OKW, or High Command of the Armed Forces), which meant that any decision to commit it to action rested with Hitler himself. Nevertheless, by June 1944 two of its components – the superbly equipped Panzer Lehr Division and the almost equally powerful 12th SS Panzer Division *Hitlerjugend* – were stationed within a day's (motorised) march of the Calvados beaches. Provided Hitler made his decision immediately he learned of the invasion, they might still intervene in time to tip the balance in the Germans' favour.

Between late 1943 and mid-1944 the combat power, fighting spirit and tactical proficiency of the *Westheer* rose significantly. Nevertheless, serious problems remained. At the higher levels command and control was confused and contradictory. German air and naval forces (the former including paratroop and infantry divisions, as well as anti-aircraft and other units) often followed directives from their own general staffs, rather than the commanders in whose areas they were stationed. The military governors in France and the Low Countries, as well as a range of Nazi Party, police and civilian agencies, also proved difficult to subordinate to direct Army control. Finally, a tense relationship existed between the *Waffen-SS* and the *Heer* (the German Army). Since the SS possessed some of the most powerful fighting units in the west, this did not bode well for an especially rapid and effective response when the invasion came.

The Germans also faced tactical and operational difficulties. Despite their reinforcement, in June 1944 the troops in the threatened areas were still over-extended and under-protected. Ammunition and fuel stocks were low, and significant damage to the transport infrastructure (caused mainly by Allied air attacks) meant that prospects for re-supply by rail looked bleak. This would have mattered less if the *Wehrmacht* had been fully motorised, but the *Westheer* was very weak in motor transport. Even the panzer divisions had only about half the trucks they were supposed to possess. It was therefore doubtful that enough men and equipment could be sent sufficiently quickly to throw the Allies back into the sea if they established a beachhead.

This did not mean the Germans were doomed to defeat. If they identified the time and place of the invasion just 24 hours before it began, local reserves could still be pushed into the front line and mobile forces moved to counter-attack positions. Then, provided all services exerted themselves to the utmost, the Allies could be repelled. If the contest became an attritional one on land, however, based more on the two sides' ability to re-supply and reinforce than on tactical skill, the Allies would hold most of the advantages. In the final analysis, the destiny of the Nazi regime depended primarily on a remarkably small number of men (probably not more than 10,000 soldiers), deployed in and around some 50 *Widerstandsnester* and *Stützpunkte* along parts of the Lower Normandy coastline. About 2,000 of these troops were in the area around Arromanches, Asnelles and Ver-sur-Mer. If they stood firm and bought enough time for others to come to their aid, the invasion might yet fail. If they did not, the collapse of the *Westheer* – and the Third Reich – seemed inevitable.

CHAPTER 2

THE ATTACKERS

By August 1943 the Western Allies were resolved on an invasion of north-west Europe, and had chosen Lower Normandy for its location. Calvados, in particular, appeared well suited to their purposes. Its firm, wide beaches offered convenient places for an amphibious landing. The region was in range of continuous air cover from England, and near enough to allow prompt reinforcement and re-supply. Cherbourg, at the head of the Cotentin peninsula, provided a large port within striking distance of the assault area, and other major harbours were relatively close by, in Brittany. Adequate lines of communication led inland, and there were appropriate places for airfield construction, especially south-east of Caen. Unlike the Pas de Calais, Lower Normandy was also relatively weakly defended. This was a critical consideration. Even if it meant covering a greater distance across the English Channel, and almost twice as far in the subsequent advance from the French coast to Germany, the improved chances of surprising the enemy and establishing a beachhead represented compelling reasons to avoid the Pas de Calais and attack Normandy instead.

The preparations for the invasion, the assault phase of which was code-named Operation 'Neptune', took many months. However, the most important aspects of the plan were developed from December 1943, when the American General Dwight D. Eisenhower was appointed Supreme Allied Commander (SAC) for the campaign in north-west Europe. Directly subordinate to Eisenhower was the Deputy SAC, the British Air Chief Marshal Sir Arthur Tedder, and the three service chiefs, who were also British.

They were Admiral Sir Bertram Ramsay (naval commander), Air Chief Marshal Sir Trafford Leigh-Mallory (air C-in-C) and General Sir Bernard Law Montgomery, former commander of the British Eighth Army in North Africa and Italy, who was given command of Allied land forces in December 1943. For initial operations the troops assigned to Montgomery included First US Army, under Lieutenant General Omar Bradley, and British Second Army, led by Lieutenant-General (Lt-Gen) Miles Dempsey. Together they formed 21st Army Group.

General Sir Bernard Montgomery. This photograph was taken on 11 June 1944, at Montgomery's first press conference in Normandy. (IWM B5337)

The participation of air and naval forces was fundamental to Operation Neptune's success. However, their main function was to create the conditions for the land battle, which alone could guarantee the Nazis' defeat. It was therefore Montgomery and his 21st Army Group staff who were primarily responsible for the strategic planning of the invasion. Like Rommel, Montgomery was convinced of the need to seize and maintain the initiative from the outset. To achieve this, he considered that the assault needed to be on a broad front and in the greatest possible strength. This would maximise the chances of gaining a firm lodgement, make it difficult for the Germans to isolate the beachhead, and facilitate a rapid advance inland. He also believed it was critical to create a solid logistical base. For this reason, although the Allies planned to take prefabricated port facilities with them (the 'Mulberry harbours'), Montgomery considered the capture of Cherbourg by First US Army a prerequisite to any significant exploitation. Finally, he thought it would be necessary to defeat determined German counter-attacks in the early stages of the invasion. Only after this was done could the Allies begin their breakout.

By May 1944 Montgomery's ideas had been translated into a detailed operational plan. This envisaged attacks

From left to right:
Lt-Gens John
Crocker, Miles
Dempsey, and
Gerard Bucknall,
photographed in
Normandy on
10 June. *(IWM
B5326)*

by US and British forces across an 80-km front, from the Cotentin peninsula in the west to the River Dives in the east. Airborne troops would land by night to secure the flanks, with seaborne forces following after dawn across a number of beaches. From west to east these were code-named 'Utah', 'Omaha', 'Gold', 'Juno' and 'Sword'. The first two were in First US Army's sector, while the others were assigned to British Second Army, which included Canadian as well as British troops. Altogether, three airborne divisions, five infantry divisions and a large number of supporting units were to land before nightfall on the opening day of the invasion.

The first task of the assault divisions was to overcome the shoreline defences and secure the main routes inland. Next, the armies would link up their beachheads (the initial attack sectors were isolated from one another by gaps of as much as 30 km) and push forward, with the aim of establishing a lodgement some 15 km deep by the end of the first day ('D-Day'). In the British sector armoured columns would also advance to seize the critical road junction of Caen and high ground near Villers-Bocage and Evrecy. These towns lay south-west of Caen, astride important lines of communication. Finally, teams of engineers would dash up to 40 km inland to blow up bridges over the River Orne south of Caen. The overall purpose was to disrupt possible counter-attacks by denying the Germans the infrastructure necessary to carry them out. For similar reasons, Montgomery wanted British Second Army to follow up its D-Day assault by a rapid thrust inland. The aim was to seize dominating terrain between Caen and Falaise, over 30 km further south. This would help protect the Americans' advance – first to Cherbourg and then south into Brittany – and result in the acquisition of an area well suited to airfield construction. It would also provide an ideal springboard for the British and Canadian break-out to the River Seine, which Montgomery hoped would occur within three months of the invasion.

To achieve his objectives, Miles Dempsey had at his disposal four corps headquarters, more than a dozen infantry and armoured divisions and many supporting units. Logistically, it would be possible to land only a fraction of these forces on D-Day. These included parts of I Corps, under Lt-Gen John Crocker, and XXX Corps, commanded by Lt-Gen Gerard Bucknall. Since I Corps was tasked with capturing Caen, Evrecy and the area north of Falaise – the lion's share of British responsibilities – it was allocated two of Second Army's three beaches. The more westerly of these, between Courseulles and St-Aubin, was 'Juno', the landing site for the Canadian 3rd Infantry Division and other units. Further east, near Ouistreham, was Sword Beach, to be attacked by the British 3rd Infantry Division and supporting forces. Crocker was also given control over the British 6th Airborne Division for the opening stages of the battle. Its intended zone of operations was east of the River Orne, on the extreme left flank of the invasion.

Bridging the gap between Crocker's corps and First US Army was XXX Corps, which was to land on Gold Beach. This extended for 18 km from Port-en-Bessin in the west to la Rivière in the east. Because more than half of this coastline was cliffs, no landing was proposed in its western and central sectors (code-named 'How' and 'Item'). Instead, XXX Corps' assault troops would go ashore on the eastern part of Gold Beach, on a 5-km frontage between le Hamel (the name given to the seafront part of Asnelles) and la Rivière. This area

General Montgomery (*right*) and Maj-Gen Douglas Graham confer in a Normandy orchard, 10 June 1944. (*IWM B5310*)

included 'Jig' and 'King' sectors, which appeared to provide exactly the type of beach required to land such a large force. Although the marshes behind the beach would be a considerable barrier to movement inland, aerial reconnaissance revealed several tracks across them, as well as reasonable roads leading south through Asnelles and Ver-sur-Mer. If these could be captured, XXX Corps would be able to push on to its objectives soon after the invasion began.

Assuming it penetrated the coastal defences, XXX Corps' next task was to link up with US V Corps on its right and the Canadians on its left, and thrust inland. By the end of D-Day the aim was to secure the town of Bayeux, 8 km from the coast, and the high ground to the south and south-east. This would have the effect of cutting the Bayeux–Caen highway (the N13), thus hindering German attempts to counter-attack. Simultaneously, mobile spearheads would rush forward to seize the dominating terrain near Villers-Bocage, 30 km from Gold Beach. These troops would be reinforced the following day, and relieved by XXX Corps' 7th Armoured Division by D+4. Having helped to paralyse German movement, Bucknall's forces would then advance further south still. If all went well, and I Corps' advance to Falaise progressed satisfactorily, within a few weeks Montgomery hoped to create the conditions for a major victory.

Leading XXX Corps' assault would be 50th (Northumbrian) Infantry Division, also known as the 'Tyne-Tees Division', after the rivers of north-east England, the area where it was originally recruited. This combat-hardened formation had seen service in North Africa and Sicily before returning to England in November 1943. On D-Day, it was commanded by Major-General (Maj-Gen) Douglas Graham, an experienced and highly decorated regular officer from the Cameronians (Scottish Rifles) who had been appointed to lead 50th Division in January 1944. Tough, capable and courageous, he embodied the qualities that Montgomery believed would be essential in the campaign.

According to the plans produced by Graham's staff, on D-Day 50th Division would land on a two-brigade frontage east of Arromanches. One infantry brigade (231st Brigade) would assault Jig sector, immediately east of le Hamel. The other (69th Brigade) was to disembark on King sector, near la Rivière. Each brigade would attack with two infantry battalions, supported by armour and engineers, with a third battalion landing in reserve. After overrunning the shoreline defences, these troops would press inland to seize the high ground overlooking the beaches. 231st Brigade would then advance west to capture Arromanches and the coastal battery at Longues, and to link up with the US V Corps, landing over 15 km away on Omaha Beach. It would be assisted by 47 Royal Marine (RM) Commando, which was to land in 231st Brigade's sector and infiltrate across

Private Arthur Twiggs of the Green Howards with his PIAT (Projector Infantry Anti-Tank) aboard a landing ship just before D-Day. The PIAT fired a 1.1 kg anti-tank grenade to a range of about 150 metres. *(IWM B5240)*

ORDER OF BATTLE: 50TH (NORTHUMBRIAN) INFANTRY DIVISION
6 June 1944

General Officer Commanding — **Maj-Gen D.A.H. Graham**
GSO 1 — *Lt-Col R.L.G. Charles*

69th Infantry Brigade — **Brigadier F.Y.C. Knox**
5th Battalion, East Yorkshire Regiment — *Lt-Col G.W. White*
6th Battalion, Green Howards — *Lt-Col R.H.W.S. Hastings*
7th Battalion, Green Howards — *Lt-Col P.H. Richardson*

151st Infantry Brigade — **Brigadier R.H. Senior**
6th Battalion, Durham Light Infantry — *Lt-Col A.E. Green*
8th Battalion, Durham Light Infantry — *Lt-Col R.P. Lidwill*
9th Battalion, Durham Light Infantry — *Lt-Col H.R. Woods*

231st Infantry Brigade — **Brigadier Sir A.B.G. Stanier**
1st Battalion, Hampshire Regiment — *Lt-Col H.D.Nelson-Smith*
1st Battalion, Dorsetshire Regiment — *Lt-Col E.A.M. Norie*
2nd Battalion, Devonshire Regiment — *Lt-Col C.A.R. Nevill*

Reconnaissance
61st Reconnaissance Regiment, RAC — *Lt-Col Sir W.M. Mount*

Machine-Gun and Heavy Mortar battalion
2nd Battalion, Cheshire Regiment — *Lt-Col S.V. Keeling*

Royal Artillery — **Brigadier C.H. Norton**
90th Field Regiment — *Lt-Col I.G.S. Hardie*
102nd Anti-Tank Regiment — *Lt-Col A.K. Matthews*
25th Light Anti-Aircraft Regiment — *Lt-Col G.G.O. Lyons*

Royal Engineers — **Lt-Col R.L. Willott**
233rd Field Company — *Major J.R. Cave-Browne*
295th Field Company — *Major C.W. Wood*
505th Field Company — *Major C.A.O.B. Compton*
235th Field Park Company — *Major I.L. Smith*

Royal Signals — **Lt-Col G.B. Stevenson**

Royal Electrical and Mechanical Engineers **Lt-Col E.H. Rundle**
69th, 151st and 231st Brigade Workshop Companies

Royal Army Service Corps — *Lt-Col G.W. Fenton*
346th, 508th, 522nd and 524th Companies

Royal Army Ordnance Corps — *Major D.C.H. Merrill*
69th, 151st and 231st Brigade Workshop Sections

Royal Army Medical Corps
149th, 186th and 200th Field Ambulances

Military Police
50th Division Provost Company — *Captain W.R. Hunter*

Formations attached to 50th Division for the assault

56th Infantry Brigade — ***Brigadier E.C. Pepper***
2nd Battalion, Essex Regiment — *Lt-Col J.F. Higson*
2nd Battalion, Gloucestershire Regiment — *Lt-Col D.W. Biddle*
2nd Battalion, South Wales Borderers — *Lt-Col R.W. Craddock*

8th Armoured Brigade — ***Brigadier H.J.B. Cracroft***
Nottinghamshire (Sherwood Rangers) Yeomanry
— *Lt-Col J. Anderson*
4th/7th Royal Dragoon Guards — *Lt-Col R.G.G. Byron*
24th Lancers — *Lt-Col W.A.C. Anderson*
147th Field Regiment, RA — *Lt-Col R.A. Phayre*

79th Armoured Division
HQ 6th Assault Regiment, RE
81st Assault Squadron, RE — *Major R.E. Thompstone*
82nd Assault Squadron, RE — *Major H.G.A. Elphinstone*
149th Assault Park Squadron, RE
B & C Squadrons, Westminster Dragoons, RAC
— *Lt-Col W.Y.K. Blair Oliphant*
13th and 15th Troops, C Squadron, 141st RAC

Royal Marines
No. 47 (Royal Marine) Commando — *Lt-Col C.F. Phillips*
1st RM Armoured Support Regiment — *Lt-Col S.V. Peskett*

Royal Artillery
7th Medium Regiment — *Lt-Col E.J. Stansfield*
86th Field Regiment — *Lt-Col G.D. Fanshawe*
198th & 234th Btys, 73rd Anti-Tank Regt — *Lt-Col Perry*
120th Light Anti-Aircraft Regiment — *Lt-Col J.B. Allan*
113th Heavy Anti-Aircraft Regiment
A Flight, 662 Air Observation Post Squadron

US Artillery
987th Field Artillery Battalion

Beach Group 104th Beach Sub-Area
(9th and 10th Beach Groups) — ***Colonel J.R.D. Gilbert***
2nd Btn, Hertfordshire Regt (beach security) — *Lt-Col J.R. Harper*
6th Btn, Border Regt (beach security) — *Lt-Col H.S. Cooper*
73rd Field Company, RE — *Major L.E. Wyatt*
89th Field Company, RE — *Major A.A. Gray*
280th Field Company, RE — *Major L.S. Clayton*
75th, 173rd, 209th, 231st and 243rd Pioneer Companies
305th, 536th and 705th Companies, RASC
24th and 25th Beach Recovery Sections
240th and 243rd Beach Provost Companies
203rd Field Ambulance
25th, 31st and 32nd Field Dressing Stations

country to seize Port-en-Bessin, on the boundary between the US and British armies. Meanwhile, 69th Brigade would establish a connection with Canadian 3rd Infantry Division and push south. After crossing the River Seulles, which flowed across its axis of advance, it would secure 50th Division's left flank by occupying the high ground around the village of St-Léger, which sat astride the N13 road 7 km south-east of Bayeux.

To fill the gap between 231st and 69th Brigades, which would be advancing on diverging axes, two additional infantry brigades were to disembark on Gold Beach shortly after the initial attack. These were 56th Brigade, which was to land on Jig sector, and 151st Brigade, which would come ashore on King. After assembling and being reinforced by armour and other units, they would move inland. 56th Brigade's objective was Bayeux and the north–south ridgeline to its west. 151st Brigade was to attack into the gap between Bayeux and 69th Brigade's sector. By the end of D-Day it was to capture the dominating ground between the River Aure, which flowed northwards through Bayeux, and the River Seulles, which ran parallel to the Aure 4 km further east. With the division's objectives secured by nightfall, its supporting armour could be released to spearhead the drive to Villers-Bocage, the next critical element in XXX Corps' plan.

The core of 50th Division lay in its infantry brigades. Each of these contained three battalions, organised into four rifle companies and a support company apiece. Each battalion comprised approximately 800 officers and men. The various battalions are listed in the box on pp. 36–7.

As well as its infantry brigades, the Tyne-Tees Division incorporated a number of other combat units. These included three field artillery regiments, one of which (90th Field Regiment) was self-propelled; 102nd Anti-Tank Regiment (Northumberland Hussars); and 25th Light Anti-Aircraft Regiment. Additional firepower was provided by 2nd Battalion, The Cheshire Regiment, the division's machine-gun and mortar battalion. There was also 61st Reconnaissance Regiment equipped with armoured cars,

plus substantial transport, workshop and engineer units. Including signals, administrative and other service elements, total divisional strength amounted to over 18,000 men.

The 50th Division was a powerful formation. Nevertheless, from early in the planning it was obvious that it lacked sufficient forces to achieve all its D-Day objectives. Consequently, in February 1944 Graham requested that three more infantry battalions should come under his command for the assault phase. Shortly after, 56th Brigade was attached to his division. To help 50th Division's thrust inland, the entire 8th Armoured Brigade was also made available. (Both of these brigades are also detailed on pp. 36–7.) Further elements added to the division's order of battle included another self-propelled artillery regiment (86th Field Regiment, The Hertfordshire Yeomanry), and, in a rare example of Anglo-American force integration, a unit of US 155-mm self-propelled guns (987th Field Artillery Battalion).

British Second Army's intention was for the landings on Gold and Sword beaches to begin at 0725 hours (H-Hour), on a rising half-tide (the assault on Juno began slightly later). The purpose was to leave the German beach obstacles exposed, so as to minimise the losses to landing craft. This meant that the leading infantry would have to cross several hundred metres of open sand before they could attack the strongpoints at the top of the beach. Clearly, this involved the risk of heavy casualties. Furthermore, as the tide rose, the beach obstacles would quickly become submerged, causing problems for follow-on

61st Reconnaissance Regiment armoured cars during training. The Humber on the left was armed with a 37-mm gun and had a maximum road speed of 70 km/hr. Note the chaplain in the light reconnaissance car. (IWM H29281)

forces as they came ashore. Under such circumstances, it was not impossible that the invasion might dissolve into chaos and disaster from the outset.

The British devised several measures to protect their assault infantry, and to facilitate successful landings by the follow-on forces. One of the most innovative lay in the use of amphibious armour. Known as DD (Duplex Drive) tanks, these were ordinary Sherman tanks fitted with propellers and a raised canvas screen, which displaced enough water to allow the vehicle to float. Off-loaded from landing craft several kilometres offshore, they were to 'swim' to the beach under their own power. Because of their low freeboard, it was anticipated that the Germans would not notice them until they emerged from the shallows, where their screens would be collapsed, allowing the tanks to fulfil their

GOLD BEACH BREACHING SQUADRONS

Jig Sector

Commanders:
Major H. Elphinstone, RE
Captain H. Stanyon, Westminster Dragoons

Composition: Two squadrons, each of three breaching teams (6 vehicles per team)
  20 AVREs from 82nd Assault Squadron, 6th Assault Regiment, RE
  (6 gun tanks, 6 bobbins, 6 fascines, 1 bridge layer, 1 command tank)
  13 Crabs from B Squadron, Westminster Dragoons
  (1 command and 12 gun tanks)
  2 armoured D7 bulldozers from 149th Sddsult Psrk Squadron, RE
  1 unarmoured D4 bulldozer from 235th Field Park Company, RE.

Attached: 73rd Field Company, RE (Major L. Wyatt, 145 officers and men)
  LCOCUs 9 and 10 (18 naval officers and ratings)

King Sector

Commanders:
Major R. Thompstone, RE
Major S. Sutton, Westminster Dragoons

Composition: As Jig sector
  AVREs from 81st Assault Squadron, 6th Assault Regiment, RE
  Crabs from C Squadron, Westminster Dragoons
  Bulldozers as Jig sector

Attached: 280th Field Company, RE (*Major L. Clayton*, 145 officers and men)
  LCOCUs 3 and 4 (18 naval officers and ratings)

normal role. If all went according to plan, the DD tanks would reach the beach a few minutes before the infantry, to provide covering fire while the infantry stormed the strongpoints. Having played their part in the destruction of the *Widerstandsnester*, the tanks would then accompany the assault brigades inland. Altogether, 76 Shermans were converted to the DD role for 50th Division's attack. They included B and C Squadrons, Sherwood Rangers, which would support 231st Brigade, and B and C Squadrons, 4th/7th RDG, which were to help 69th Brigade.

Further assistance was provided by the specialised vehicles of 79th Armoured Division. These were assembled into 'breaching squadrons', four of which were to land on Jig and King just before the infantry. Their role was to help penetrate the defences and to assist the follow-on forces by clearing obstacles and minefields. Each squadron comprised a mix of Sherman Crabs, Armoured Vehicles Royal Engineers (AVREs) and bulldozers. The Crabs were converted Sherman tanks, which used a rotating drum fitted with chains to flail the ground and detonate mines as the vehicle moved forward. On Gold Beach, the Crabs were from B and C Squadrons, Westminster Dragoons. The AVREs were converted Churchill tanks, manned by Royal Engineers from 6th Assault Regiment. In place of their main armament, each had a 290-mm spigot mortar, which was used to fire a demolition projectile (or 'petard')

Royal Navy demolition teams were among the first personnel to disembark on Gold Beach. Here, frogmen from a LCOCU train on a model of an 'Element C' obstacle in a swimming pool somewhere in the UK. *(IWM MH15649)*

41

FORCE G NAVAL CRAFT FOR LANDINGS TO GOLD BEACH
(principal units only)

Commander: _Commodore C.E. Douglas-Pennant, RN_   HMS _Bulolo_

Assault Group G1   _Captain J.W. Farquhar, RN_   HMS _Nith_
Carrying 231st Brigade   _Brigadier Sir A. Stanier_

Landing Ships Infantry – Large _[LSI(L)], troop transports, carrying_
Landing Craft Assault [LCA]

SS _Empire Arquebus_	18 LCA (524th Flotilla)
SS _Empire Crossbow_	18 LCA (553rd Flotilla)
SS _Empire Spearhead_	18 LCA (525th Flotilla)
HMS _Glenroy_	11 LCA (554th Flotilla),
	12 LCA (559th Flotilla)

Landing Craft Headquarters _[LCH]_
 LCH 100 and _LCH 317_

'D' Landing Craft Tank Squadron _(LCT; including attached elements)_

15th LCT Flotilla	12 LCT(3)
23rd LCT Flotilla	10 LCT(4)
28th LCT Flotilla	12 LCT(4)
33rd LCT Flotilla	17 LCT(4)
49th LCT Flotilla (2nd Div)	5 LCT(4)
53rd LCT Flotilla	10 LCT(4)
55th LCT Flotilla (2nd Div)	5 LCT(4)

Support Squadron

332nd Support Flotilla	3 Landing Craft Flak _[LCF(4)]_,
	3 Landing Craft Gun – Large _[LCG(L)]_
108th LCT(A) Flotilla	8 Landing Craft Tank (Armoured) _[LCT(A)]_
322nd LCT(R) Flotilla	4 Landing Craft Tank – Rocket _[LCT(R)]_
591st Assault Flotilla	9 Landing Craft Assault (Hedgerow) _[LCA(HR)]_

Assault Group G2   _Captain F.A. Balance, RN_   HMS _Kingsmill_
Carrying 69th Brigade Brigadier F. Knox

Landing Ships Infantry – Large

SS _Empire Halberd_	16 LCA (539th Flotilla)
SS _Empire Lance_	17 LCA (540th Flotilla)
SS _Empire Mace_	18 LCA (541st Flotilla)
SS _Empire Rapier_	18 LCA (542nd Flotilla)

Landing Craft Headquarters
 LCH 187 and _LCH 275_

'L' Landing Craft Tank Squadron _(including attached elements)_

12th LCT Flotilla	12 LCT(3)
24th LCT Flotilla	12 LCT(4)
34th LCT Flotilla	12 LCT(4)
49th LCT Flotilla (1st Div)	5 LCT(4)
51st LCT Flotilla	12 LCT(4)
55th LCT Flotilla (1st Div)	5 LCT(4)

Support Squadron

332nd Support Flotilla	4 LCF(4), 3 LCG(L)
109th LCT(A) Flotilla	8 LCT(A)
322nd LCT(R) Flotilla	4 LCT(R)
591st Assault Flotilla	9 LCA(HR)

Assault Group G3 *Capt G.V.M. Dolphin, RN* HMS *Albrighton*

Carrying 151st Brigade — **Brigadier R. Senior**
56th Brigade — **Brigadier E. Pepper**

Landing Craft Infantry – Large

264th Flotilla (Canadian)	6 LCI(L)
61st Division (US)	6 LCI(L)
62nd Division (US)	6 LCI(L)
70th Division (US)	3 LCI(L)

Landing Ships Tank

22nd Division (US)	6 LST
55th Division (US)	6 LST
56th Division (US)	5 LST
65th Division (US)	6 LST
101st Division (US)	6 LST

at bunkers and obstacles. Most AVREs also carried additional equipment. Some were fitted with fascines (compressed bundles of brushwood, which could be dropped into craters or anti-tank ditches to facilitate a crossing); others carried detachable bridges. Following a daring reconnaissance by Combined Operations Pilotage Parties frogmen in December 1943, which revealed patches of soft clay on the shore between Asnelles and la Rivière, 12 AVREs were also fitted with 'bobbins'. These were 75-metre lengths of steel and fabric matting, wound on a drum attached to the front of the AVRE, which could be laid like a carpet to prevent vehicles bogging down. Last, the Gold Beach breaching squadrons included two Royal Engineer field companies. Together with naval frogmen from the Landing Craft Obstacle Clearance Units (LCOCUs), they were to use explosives to clear lanes through the obstacles before the arrival of the reserve brigades and follow-on forces.

LCT(R) 440, which supported 69th Brigade's assault. (IWM B5263)

To maximise the chances of a successful landing, 50th Division would also benefit from massive fire support. Some of this was to be provided by units under Graham's direct command. These included 86th, 90th and 147th Field Regiments, each of which had 24 Sexton self-propelled 25-pounder guns which could fire from their landing craft while approaching the beach. So could 1st Royal Marine Armoured Support Regiment's 32 Centaur tanks, each of which mounted a 95-mm howitzer. Attached to 50th Division to provide even more firepower, these were to land beside the breaching squadrons from specially adapted Landing Craft Tank (Armoured) – LCT(A)s – and give direct fire support to the infantry until the shoreline defences were neutralised.

Yet more fire support came from the air and sea. In the final 30 minutes before touch-down, 43 squadrons of US heavy bombers (B-17s from Eighth Air Force's 1st Bombardment Division) were to strike at the Gold Beach defences. Further assistance was to be provided by RAF Bomber Command, which would attack German coastal batteries a few hours earlier, and by the fighter-bombers of the RAF's Second Tactical Air Force, which would strafe targets inland and be on call throughout D-Day. Aerial observers would also play a critical role in directing the fire of Bombarding Force K, which was one of five naval task forces established to support the landings. Force K consisted of four Royal Navy cruisers, a Dutch gunboat and 13 destroyers. Sitting close offshore, their role was to

A knocked out Sherman Crab (note the rotating drum and heavy chains) on Gold Beach. In the background is a bogged DD tank. (IWM B5141)

shell pre-identified coastal batteries, resistance nests and other targets in the Gold Beach area for up to two hours before the assault began. They would be supported by eight rocket-firing Landing Craft Tank (Rocket) [LCT(R) s] and over 40 other converted landing craft, mounting artillery pieces, mortars and automatic weapons. A few minutes before the landings started these vessels were to approach the coast and drench the beach obstacles and strongpoints with fire. Later, they were to provide direct support when requested to do so. For this purpose, four Landing Craft Headquarters (LCH) would be stationed offshore, linked by radio to the assault battalions and the supporting naval vessels. Among the attacking troops there would also be 13 Forward Observer, Bombardment (FOB) parties to direct naval fire support against targets inland. If the communications system worked as it was supposed to, it would be possible to support 50th Division all the way to its D-Day objectives, and beyond.

During early 1944, 50th Division and its attached units undertook intensive preparations for the D-Day assault. New equipment was received, and a considerable number of reinforcements and replacements absorbed. In February the division's personnel were introduced to the specialised assault equipment of 79th Armoured Division, with which they trained in various tactical scenarios. Subsequently, the assault brigades spent several weeks at No. 1 Combined Operations Training Centre, on the shores of Loch Fyne in Scotland. Here they re-acquainted themselves with the techniques of the amphibious assault, before moving with the rest of the division to the south coast of England for a series of exercises and rehearsals. These were carried out in co-operation with Naval Force G, which was formed on 1 March 1944 to carry 50th Division across the Channel. Four brigade-sized exercises took place during April, followed at the start of May by Exercise Fabius. This involved all of 50th Division in an amphibious landing on Hayling Island, near Portsmouth, and was in effect a dress rehearsal for the assault. Following its completion, Force G returned to port to overhaul and refit its vessels. Maj-Gen Graham's division also went back to its camps in and around the New Forest, spending the next four weeks water-proofing its vehicles and carrying out other pre-invasion tasks. These included the production of brigade and battalion operation orders, and the briefing of all ranks on their role on D-Day. For this purpose, extensive use was made of air photographs, models and dummy maps (accurate maps of the invasion area, on which the real place names were replaced for security reasons with false ones).

At 2359 hours on 25 May the camps holding the British assault forces were sealed, signalling the final phase of the pre-invasion preparations. On 31 May, 231st Brigade moved to Southampton to embark on the large Landing Ships Infantry (LSIs) that were to carry it to Normandy. It was followed later the same day by 69th Brigade, and on 3 June by 151st and 56th Brigades, which embarked at Lymington and Southampton in Canadian and US Landing Craft Infantry (Large) [LCI(L)s]. Meanwhile, the specialised assault equipment of 79th Armoured Division and the DD tanks of 4th/7th RDG and the Sherwood Rangers – all of which were highly secret – were taken aboard their Landing Craft Tank (LCTs) at Stanswood Bay, a secluded location well away from the hurly-burly of Southampton Docks. Then, together with the rest of the Force G armada, they moved into the Solent to await the order to sail. The long-desired liberation of north-west Europe was about to begin.

Force G landing craft at Southampton, 1 June. In the centre are *LCH 100* and *LCH 317*, which served as headquarters vessels for the landing on Jig sector. Also visible are LCT(3)s from 15th Flotilla, which carried the DD Shermans of the Sherwood Rangers, and the larger LCT(4)s of 23rd Flotilla. (IWM EA 23731)

CHAPTER 3

D-DAY: THE ASSAULT

Shortly after 0700 hours on Monday 5 June, the first elements of Force G left their anchorage in the Solent and departed for France. They included the breaching squadron LCTs, as well as the armoured landing craft of 108th and 109th LCT(A) Flotillas, carrying the Royal Marine Centaurs. They were followed by a succession of vessels, among them 12th and 15th LCT Flotillas, with the DD tanks of 4th/7th RDG and Sherwood Rangers aboard, and 24th, 33rd and 49th LCT Flotillas, which carried 50th Division's self-propelled artillery. Owing to their much faster speed, the eight LSIs which were to take the two assault brigades across the Channel did not raise anchor until 1830 hours. They were accompanied by HMS *Bulolo*, a converted merchant vessel generously equipped with radios and other command facilities, serving as Force G's headquarters ship. The LSIs were followed by 22 American LSTs (Landing Ships Tank). These carried hundreds of vehicles, among them the 61 Shermans from 24th Lancers, the only one of 8th Armoured Brigade's regiments not equipped with DD tanks. The LSTs also towed 13 rhino ferries, powered rafts designed to shuttle equipment between the landing ships and the beach. Last to depart were the 19 LCI(L)s carrying the reserve brigades, which slipped their moorings at Southampton between 1900 and 2000 hours.

The Allies hoped to surprise the Germans, and thereby to avoid air and sea attacks on their assault convoys. Nevertheless, in addition to remote screening by warships

Maj-Gen Graham observes the landings from HMS *Bulolo* on the morning of 6 June. *(IWM A23881)*

NAVAL BOMBARDMENT OF GOLD BEACH DEFENCES

Bombarding Force K

Ship	Main armament	Principal target
HMS *Argonaut* (cruiser)	10 x 5.25-in	105-mm bty, Vaux (WN-50)
HMS *Ajax* (cruiser)	8 x 6-in	150-mm bty, Longues
HMS *Orion* (cruiser)	8 x 6-in	122-mm bty, Mont Fleury
HMS *Emerald* (cruiser)	7 x 6-in	105-mm bty (WN-41)
HMNS *Flores* (gunboat)[1]	3 x 5.9-in	Gun position (WN-39)
HMS *Grenville* (destroyer)	4 x 4.7-in	Jig sector beach defences
HMS *Jervis* (destroyer)	6 x 4.7-in	Jig sector beach defences
HMS *Ulster* (destroyer)	4 x 4.7-in	King sector beach defences
HMS *Ulysses* (destroyer)	4 x 4.7-in	Jig sector beach defences
HMS *Undaunted* (destroyer)	4 x 4.7-in	King sector beach defences
HMS *Undine* (destroyer)	4 x 4.7-in	Jig sector beach defences
HMS *Urania* (destroyer)	4 x 4.7-in	Jig sector beach defences
HMS *Urchin* (destroyer)	4 x 4.7-in	King sector beach defences
HMS *Ursa* (destroyer)	4 x 4.7-in	King sector beach defences
HMS *Cattistock* (destroyer)	4 x 4-in	King sector beach defences
HMS *Cottesmore* (destroyer)	4 x 4-in	King sector beach defences
HMS *Pytchley* (destroyer)	4 x 4-in	King sector beach defences
ORP *Krakowiak* (destroyer)[2]	6 x 4-in	King sector beach defences

Bombarding Force E[3]

HMS *Belfast* (cruiser)	12 x 6-in	100-mm bty, Ver (WN-32)

Field Regiments[4] and Principal Small Craft

86th Field Regiment	24 x 25-pdr	King sector beach defences
90th Field Regiment	24 x 25-pdr	Jig sector beach defences
147th Field Regiment	24 x 25-pdr[5]	Jig sector beach defences
LCG(L) 1, 2, 3	2 x 4.7-in[6]	King sector beach defences
LCG(L) 13, 17, 18	2 x 4.7-in[6]	Jig sector beach defences
LCT(R) 362, 440, 459, 460	5-in rockets[7]	King sector beach defences
LCT(R) 434, 435, 436, 438	5-in rockets[7]	Jig sector beach defences

Notes

1. Dutch.
2. Polish.
3. Bombarding Force E supported the Juno Beach landings. However, because WN-32 was in the Gold Beach sector, HMS Belfast's contribution is recorded here.
4. Firing from LCTs during run-in.
5. Only 20 guns fired.
6. Per craft.
7. Approximately 1,000 rockets per craft.

and aircraft, Force G had its own escort. This included fighter cover, as well as the ships of Bombarding Force K. Sixteen other vessels participated, among them Royal Navy sloops and armed trawlers, plus two Free French frigates and two Greek corvettes. Smaller vessels included 14 launches, whose job it was to guide the transports, and a dozen motor torpedo boats. Operating ahead of Force G were more than 30 minesweepers, clearing channels through the German mine barrier that was known to exist north of the invasion area.

Force G's crossing took place in difficult weather conditions. Owing to a decision by General Eisenhower to delay the invasion by a day, the worst ravages of a storm that passed through the Channel on the night of 4–5 June were avoided. As it emerged around the western end of the Isle of Wight, however, Force G was buffeted by strong winds and choppy waves. Many of the troops on board the LCTs spent a miserable 24 hours in partly flooded vessels, and seasickness was common, even on the larger transports. Two flotillas of small landing craft, which were intended to ferry the reserve brigades from the LCI(L)s to shore, were forced by the rough weather to turn back to the English coast. So were at least four of the 16 LCT(A)s. Owing to their low freeboard and indifferent construction, these landing craft proved especially vulnerable to the heavy seas. One capsized, and although most of the others pressed on, the two LCT(A) flotillas fell badly behind schedule. Equally serious, six out of 18 Landing Craft Assault, Hedgerow [LCA(HR)] were swamped and sank. Although a minor loss in numerical terms, the unavailability of these boats, which were to clear lanes through the beach obstacles by firing salvoes of mortar bombs, represented a not insignificant reduction in the capabilities of the assault waves.

Aboard the LSIs, by contrast, the troops of 231st and 69th Brigades had an incident-free crossing. After messages of encouragement from Eisenhower, Montgomery and Graham had been read to them over the ships' broadcasting systems, many retired to their bunks. Meanwhile, officers and NCOs pored over the latest maps and air photographs, or tried to get a few hours sleep. At 0300 hours on 6 June, while Force G was still in mid-Channel, reveille was sounded. Those who could face eating enjoyed an early breakfast, while others managed only their anti-seasickness tablets and rum ration. At about 0500 hours, the infantry

Very few photographs survive of the Gold Beach assault troops. This picture shows men of 1st Dorsets, plus three beach group personnel (identifiable by the white band around each of their helmets), aboard an LCA shortly before H-Hour. (Devon & Dorset Regiment Museum)

companies began forming into individual craft loads on the troop decks. A few minutes later the LSIs dropped anchor 12 km from the Calvados coast, and started to lower their Landing Craft Assault (LCA) into the cold and turbulent waters of the Bay of the Seine. These were the boats, each carrying around 30 men, which would deliver the leading battalions to their destinations on Gold Beach.

At 0530 hours, as 231st and 69th Brigades' personnel clambered into their landing craft, the preliminary bombardment of the German defences began. HMS *Ajax*, targeting the Longues Battery, and HMS *Belfast*, which was tasked with neutralising the Marefontaine Battery (WN-32), were the first to contribute. They were joined minutes later by HMS *Emerald*, shelling an artillery position south of Arromanches. Gradually the rest of Force K opened fire, until by 0630 hours a hundred heavy naval guns were pounding the defences. Almost simultaneously, squadrons of US heavy bombers appeared overhead, deluging their cargoes onto the *Widerstandsnester* and the coastal batteries. With H-Hour approaching, the aircraft, cruisers and destroyers were joined by rocket-firing LCT(R)s, other support vessels and 50th Division's self-propelled guns, firing from their landing craft as they approached the beach.

The effects of the bombardment were impressive. Several German strongpoints were hit heavily, especially around

Ver-sur-Mer. The Mont Fleury Battery was suppressed, with hardly a round fired by any of its guns. Although casualty figures are not known, many of Ver's defenders were thrown into shock. This was particularly true of the garrisons of WN-34, at the Mont Fleury lighthouse, and WN-32, near Marefontaine farm. Most of the personnel of 441st *Ost* Battalion also appear to have had their fighting spirit shattered by the bombardment. Further west, in 352nd Division's sector, serious damage was done to the Longues Battery. Here, accurate overnight bombing was followed by some remarkable shooting by HMS *Ajax*, which put 6-inch rounds through the embrasures of two of the 150-mm gun casemates. Although the Longues Battery maintained a sporadic fire thereafter, it posed little threat during the rest of D-Day.

The bombardment, however, did not go entirely to plan. Smoke and dust occasionally obscured targets, forcing temporary interruptions to the naval gunfire. Cloud cover was also much thicker than anticipated, causing entire squadrons to bomb inaccurately. Consequently, many positions were only slightly damaged. Among them were WN-39, which overlooked Jig sector, and WN-35, at the western end of King sector. Nor were the *Widerstandsnester* in la Rivière (WN-33) and le Hamel (WN-37 and WN-38) neutralised. Control over these locations was essential to developing routes inland, and both were known to be strongly held. Yet, despite being top priority targets, the strongpoints survived. In the case of la Rivière, over 1,000 4.7-inch shells, 2,000 5-inch rockets and large quantities of lighter ordnance were aimed at WN-33 before H-Hour. Nevertheless, its massively constructed 88-mm gun casemate suffered only superficial damage, and the garrison emerged from their shelters intact. Meanwhile WN-37, which dominated the western end of Jig sector, was barely touched. Many of the aircraft sent to attack it missed their target by several kilometres, and others dropped their bombs on the beach or offshore. The rockets fired by the LCT(R)s also appear to have fallen mainly in the sea (according to one report, several landed among the breaching team LCTs).

ALL LOOTERS WILL BE SHOT   YOU HAVE BEEN WARNED

This photo shows *LCT 886*, heavily damaged while attempting to land its breaching team at le Hamel, and which eventually drifted ashore near WN-36. A hedgehog obstacle (with shell still attached) can be seen on the beach at left. *(IWM A23948)*

Finally, because of problems with its control craft, 147th Field Regiment was unable to fire on le Hamel during its run-in, as intended. Instead, it joined 90th Field Regiment in bombarding WN-36, over 500 metres further east. This meant that WN-36 was smothered with high explosive, but the defenders of WN-37 were left almost totally unscathed.

At approximately 0600 hours, the assault battalions' LCAs began their run-in. In front of them sailed the breaching team LCTs and surviving LCA(HR)s, while behind came the self-propelled artillery regiments. These were followed by more LCAs, carrying 231st and 69th Brigades' reserve battalions. Absent, however, were most of the LCT(A)s, as well as the DD tanks. Because of the heavy seas, a decision was taken not to risk launching these, but to land them in shallow water instead. This worked well on King sector, where 4th/7th RDG disembarked alongside the breaching squadrons. However, on Jig sector the revised plan miscarried. Here, owing to insufficient sea-room, 15th LCT Flotilla's run-in was badly delayed. Rather than landing its 38 Shermans at 0720 hours, as originally intended, the first of the Sherwood Rangers' tanks did not go ashore until 0758. Consequently, for the first half an hour of its battle, 231st Brigade fought without any support from its two DD squadrons.

JIG SECTOR

According to 50th Division's plan, in the absence of the amphibious armour and Centaurs, the attack on Jig sector was to begin with the arrival of the breaching squadrons at 0725 hours. They would be followed seven minutes later by the leading elements of the assault battalions. These included 1st Hampshires, which was to land close to le Hamel on Jig Green West, and 1st Dorsets, disembarking opposite WN-36 on Jig Green East. Both units would land their A and B Companies first, together with part of their support companies and the assault engineers of 295th Field Company (known rather colourfully as 'thug parties'). They would be followed 13 minutes later by their C and D Companies, battalion headquarters and more engineers. Accompanying them would be members of the Beach Group, including naval signallers and the principal beachmaster (also a naval officer), whose role it was to co-ordinate the disembarkation of the follow-on forces. At 0810 hours (H+45) 2nd Devons, 231st Brigade's reserve battalion, would arrive to give additional impetus to the attack. The first self-propelled guns were expected at H+60, and by 0900 hours it was anticipated that the beach would be a hive of activity, as further combat and support elements landed. Among them would be the non-DD tanks of the Sherwood Rangers (A Squadron), more artillery (some of it anti-tank or anti-aircraft) and many of 231st Brigade's vehicles. If everything went to schedule, the three battalions of 56th Brigade were due to disembark soon after 1000 hours.

Once ashore, the leading infantry companies, assisted by the breaching teams, were to capture the beach defences (WN-36, WN-37 and WN-38) and the village of Asnelles, which dominated the existing routes inland. This would allow the assault battalions to thrust west and south-west to seize the high ground overlooking Jig, and to overcome the German positions around Arromanches. Meanwhile, 2nd Devons was to advance down the valley of la Gronde Ruisseau (la Gronde Riviere [sic] on Allied 1944 maps) to occupy Ryes, opening the road to Bayeux for exploitation by 56th Brigade. Thereafter, 231st Brigade would attack west to capture the Longues Battery and link up with US forces approaching from Omaha. Spearheading the advance would be 47 RM Commando, which was to land on Jig sector around 0930 hours. Its task was to capture Port-en-Bessin, on the extreme right flank of Second Army's area. To achieve this, it would move across country to a dominating terrain feature (known as Point 72, but Point 64 on modern maps) near Escures. Having established a 'firm base' there, it would then attack north to take its objective during the afternoon of D-Day.

As described in detail in Tour B (*see pp. 132–49*), 231st Brigade's landing did not go according to plan. Only two of the nine LCA(HR)s allocated to Jig sector fired as intended. Owing to the failure to neutralise WN-37, the three breaching teams assigned to Jig Green West met heavy resistance as they approached the shore. One of their LCTs was badly damaged and proved unable to disembark its vehicles and personnel, and many of the remaining AVREs and Crabs were knocked out or became bogged when they landed. Although one lane was opened through the lateral minefield at the top of the beach, German fire soon rendered it unusable. Meanwhile, most of LCOCU 10's frogmen and 73rd Field Company's assault engineers were forced to take cover in the shallows or among the sand dunes. Consequently, few of the beach obstacles – which proved more numerous and better constructed than expected – were demolished.

1st Hampshires' and 1st Dorsets' assault also failed to develop in the manner intended. Navigational errors and

A Sherman tank of the Sherwood Rangers disembarks beside a bomb crater on Jig Red soon after 0900 hours. Also visible are a 49th Flotilla LCT, an M14 half-track and an LCA. *(IWM B5258)*

the effects of the strong north-westerly wind pushed both battalions' LCAs much further east than planned. Instead of landing on Jig Green West, at 0735 hours 1st Hampshires' A Company disembarked opposite WN-36 on Jig Green East, with B Company several hundred metres to its left. 1st Dorsets, which was supposed to land in this area and capture WN-36, put its first troops ashore on Jig Red, about 1 km to the east. The same was true of the remaining breaching teams, all of which landed on Jig Red. Most of the assault battalions' reserve companies and headquarters personnel also came ashore east of their intended landing sectors.

The physical separation of the Jig Green West breaching teams and 1st Hampshires' leading companies during the critical opening minutes of the attack threw 231st Brigade's plan into disarray. Although 1st Hampshires' A Company quickly stormed and captured WN-36, when two of its platoons moved along the dunes towards their objective at le Hamel, they came under a devastating fire from WN-37. Casualties mounted rapidly, and despite reinforcement by C Company, it proved impossible to make significant progress towards the German strongpoint. Had additional firepower become available, momentum might yet have been regenerated. However, when the Sherwood Rangers' B Squadron landed at 0800 hours, three of its 19 tanks drowned, several others were knocked out and most of the remainder became stuck in clay patches on the beach. Since 1st Hampshires' mortar platoon could not be located, and contact with the supporting naval vessels had broken down, it was decided temporarily to abandon the attack on WN-37.

Attempts to penetrate the Jig sector defences were hampered by several factors, not least the disproportionately heavy losses among officers and senior NCOs during the early stages of the attack. Among the dead were the commander of 82nd Assault Squadron, RE, the commander of 1st Hampshires' A Company and several platoon leaders. Many others were badly wounded, including Lt-Col H.D. Nelson-Smith, the Hampshires' commander; the CO of the Sherwood Rangers (Lt-Col J. Anderson); and four out of five of 1st Dorsets' company sergeant-majors. This had a disruptive effect on command and control, and on unit cohesion, which was compounded by breakdowns in communication. Some of these were caused by enemy action (for example the destruction of 1st Hampshires' B Company headquarters by a German shell). Others, however, resulted from the scattering of 231st Brigade's personnel as they came ashore. For some time after landing, 2nd Devons' commander, Lt-Col C.A.R. Nevill, was unable to locate any members of his battalion; similarly, Lt-Col C.F. Phillips, CO of 47 RM Commando, did not join his own unit until the early afternoon. Nor were matters helped when Brigadier Sir Alexander Stanier's LCM (Landing Craft Mechanised) was sunk, with the loss of much brigade headquarters equipment, as it attempted to land at about 0830 hours.

By 0900 hours the situation along Jig sector appeared chaotic. Owing to the strong on-shore winds, the tide had risen faster than expected, submerging the majority of the beach obstacles before they could be demolished. This led to extensive damage to landing craft, many of which struck mines as they approached the shore. For similar reasons, only a narrow strip of sand remained for the disembarkation of follow-on forces. Of six gaps that should have been created through the lateral minefield, just two were in use. Both were on Jig Red, east of a huge bomb crater in the coastal road, which ran parallel to the beach. This crater was eventually filled by three fascines, but until this was done it caused a massive traffic jam immediately behind the seashore. Fortunately for 50th Division, the Germans failed to make the most of the resulting opportunity to cause significant losses. Nevertheless, incoming rounds from the Meuvaines area caused considerable disruption to attempts to press inland. There were also a number of casualties, among them Major A.C.W. Martin, 1st Hampshires' second-in-command, who was killed while disembarking to take over the battalion at 0930 hours.

231st Brigade's performance during the opening stages of the assault was marked by considerable gallantry, but little real progress. However, at around H+2 hours,

the brigade finally began to push towards its objectives. The key to its advance lay at WN-36, which had been captured by 1st Hampshires' A Company, and from which a sandy track led south towards Meuvaines. Soon after landing, 1st Hampshires' B Company had pushed forward along this route, occupying the farm buildings at les Roquettes, 600 metres inland. In the process, the company created a bridgehead on the southern edge of the marsh, which was reinforced over the next 90 minutes by other elements of the assault forces. Among them was the Hampshires' D Company, along with most of 1st Dorsets. With the arrival of the latter's B Company, which was responsible under 231st Brigade's plan for holding les Roquettes, it became possible to use the farm buildings as the springboard for a further attack. Consequently, at about 0915 hours, the first troops set off inland. They included 1st Hampshires' B Company, advancing towards Asnelles, and 1st Dorsets' C and D Companies, pushing around the southern edge of the village to Buhot, as a preliminary to capturing the high ground 500 metres further west. On Brigadier Stanier's personal instruction, elements of 2nd Devons also set off, moving across the open fields between Asnelles and Meuvaines. Their objective was Ryes, which Stanier was anxious to secure in order to pre-empt the arrival of German reserves from Bayeux.

231st Brigade's spearheads encountered various problems as they advanced. Despite good progress by 69th Brigade on its left, the Germans still held several

This photograph was taken around 0900 hours on Jig Red. The LCTs are from 53rd Flotilla, carrying 1st Dorsets' priority vehicles and A Squadron, Sherwood Rangers Yeomanry. Note the mine damage to the bow of LCT 858. (IWM B5244)

positions on the slopes near Meuvaines, from which they directed mortar, artillery and machine-gun fire onto the advancing troops, causing casualties. 1st Hampshires' B Company had to fight through a small German position on the eastern outskirts of Asnelles, and then became involved in the difficult and time-consuming task of neutralising pockets of resistance within the village itself. Two platoons from 1st Dorsets' C Company also found themselves engaged at the southern end of Asnelles, and spent well over an hour clearing houses before continuing towards their objective. Meanwhile, persistent communications problems meant that 2nd Devons' C and D Companies failed to receive Brigadier Stanier's order to by-pass German resistance in le Hamel. Instead, in accordance with their original instructions, the two companies moved west into the village, where they expected to find their battalion assembly area, only to become pinned down near WN-37. Although D Company managed to extricate itself at around 1100 hours, C Company's commander was killed and the company remained stuck in le Hamel. After a costly landing, during which most of its assault boats were sunk or damaged, 47 RM Commando also spent the entire morning re-organising on Jig sector, instead of advancing towards Port-en-Bessin.

Despite its difficulties, thanks to Brigadier Stanier's intervention and the initiative displayed by junior officers and NCOs, by late morning 231st Brigade was finally shaking itself free from the coastal strip. As further elements of 1st Hampshires entered Asnelles from the east, a firm foothold was established in the village. Although WN-37 and WN-38 remained in German hands, the former came

The seafront at la Rivière, looking east. The sea wall is a post-war structure, but similar to the one seen in the photo on p. 12 beneath which 5th East Yorks' D and C Companies sheltered before storming WN-33. (Author)

under increasing fire from armoured vehicles advancing along the coastal road. One of them, a self-propelled gun from 147th Field Regiment, managed to knock out the 75-mm gun at the heart of WN-37, and although movement inland remained difficult, more and more vehicles started heading into Asnelles from the north. The Royal Navy also lent useful support, bombarding gun and mortar positions at Meuvaines and near Ryes. This led to a noticeable reduction in German fire, which in turn eased the task of sorting out the chaos along the beach. Albeit two hours later than intended, almost precisely on the stroke of midday 56th Brigade's LCI(L)s beached at the eastern end of Jig Red sector. Within 30 minutes, the troops of the reserve brigade were ashore and heading inland.

KING SECTOR

As with Jig sector, the assault on King sector was timed to begin at 0725 hours, with the arrival of half a dozen LCTs, each carrying a breaching team composed of AVREs, Sherman Crabs and bulldozers. Disembarking alongside them were 4th/7th RDG's 38 DD tanks, to be joined a few minutes later by the first of the assault infantry. These included 5th East Yorks' A and D Companies, landing on King Red sector just west of la Rivière, and 6th Green Howards' A and D Companies, which would come ashore on King Green. (King Green began about 750 metres west of la Rivière, at the northern end of a track across the marshes, and extended for 1 km to the eastern boundary of Jig sector.) Reinforcing the assault infantry would be part of 6th Green Howards' and 5th East Yorks' support companies (mortarmen, signallers

Soldiers of 7th Green Howards cross King Green beach at about 0830 hours. An 81st Assault Squadron AVRE fitted with a Bobbin is visible in the surf towards the right of the photograph, as are beach obstacles (by this time becoming submerged), Sherman tanks and other vehicles. *(IWM MH2021)*

This picture, taken at approximately 0945 hours on King Green, shows the sliver of beach available for disembarkation during the three hours of high water. Visible on the right through the haze is a Sexton self-propelled gun from 86th Field Regiment (towing a 'porpoise' ammunition sled). The drowned vehicle is an M14 half-track. *(IWM MH2320)*

and pioneers), plus engineers from 233rd Field Company, who were to clear gaps through the coastal minefield. At H+20 (0745 hours) the reserve companies (B and C) and headquarters of the two leading battalions would land, followed 20 minutes later by 69th Brigade's third battalion, 7th Green Howards. It would be accompanied by three Churchill Crocodile flame-thrower tanks, four self-propelled anti-tank guns and elements of the Royal Navy Beach Commando. The reserve squadron of 4th/7th RDG was due ashore at 0825 hours, together with the tracked vehicles of the assault battalions. Having supported the initial assault from its LCTs, 86th Field Regiment's Sextons would begin disembarking just before 0900. In the absence of the small landing craft that were supposed to ferry its troops ashore, 151st Brigade's LCI(L)s were to beach on King sector about an hour later.

69th Brigade's landing area was dominated by the Meuvaines ridge, which ran roughly parallel with the coast 1 km inland. Although it was essential to neutralise the shoreline positions at both ends of King sector (WN-35 at the western extremity, and WN-33 in la Rivière), it was equally important for the assault battalions quickly to cross the marsh and seize the high ground overlooking the beach. For this reason, immediately after disembarking, 5th East Yorks' A Company was to capture the strongpoint at the Mont Fleury lighthouse (WN-34). Meanwhile, 6th Green Howards' D Company would overrun the coastal battery 600 metres further west, while its B and C Companies attacked a series of German dug-outs and fire positions along the high ground towards Meuvaines. The two assault battalions, supported by the DD squadrons, would then push inland to clear Ver-sur-Mer and Meuvaines. At this point, 7th Green Howards would also move forward, storming WN-32 and despatching a mobile column to capture the bridge across the River Seulles at Creully (where contact was to be made with Canadian 3rd Infantry Division). During the same phase, 6th Green Howards would advance to Villiers-le-Sec and establish its own bridgehead across the Seulles at St-Gabriel. Thereafter, 69th Brigade would head south to secure the high ground around St-Léger. If all went to plan, by nightfall it was hoped that all three battalions, plus various supporting arms, would be in position astride the N13 highway south-east of Bayeux.

For various reasons, the assault on King sector went considerably more smoothly than the attack on Jig. Unlike at Asnelles, the preliminary air and naval bombardment of the Ver-sur-Mer area was generally accurate and effective. Thanks to some prominent landmarks (notably the Mont Fleury lighthouse and an isolated house 600 metres further west), the assault troops landed on time and in the right locations. As a result, they were able to capitalise on the effects of the bombardment before the Germans

This remarkable photograph shows WN-33's 88-mm casemate (the squarish feature next to the beach), with British troops clustered along the seawall beneath it. Several armoured vehicles can be seen, including one crossing the coastal minefield to the road beyond. Judging by the tide, the photograph was taken before 1230 hours. *(Keele University Air Photo Archive)*

The 88-mm casemate at la Rivière (WN-33), showing the massive walls on either side of the embrasure, which protected it against observation and fire from the sea or inland. The sign at left reads 'Wheels Exit', indicating that non-tracked vehicles were to head inland from the beach at this point. (IWM A23995)

could recover. Furthermore, owing to the almost simultaneous arrival of infantry, assault engineers and tanks, something resembling the all-arms battle intended in 50th Division's plan actually materialised. Consequently, although 69th Brigade's assault was not without difficulties, within two hours of the initial landings a significant breach was created in 716th Infantry Division's defences along the eastern part of Gold Beach.

As described in detail in Tour A (*see pp. 114–31*), 6th Green Howards' attack on King Green met with rapid success. Little enemy fire was received during the run-in, and almost all the assault troops reached the top of the beach in good order. So did most of the breaching team vehicles and DD tanks. After a flurry of resistance, the *Widerstandsnest* at the western end of King sector (WN-35) was overcome by a combined assault by 6th Green Howards' A Company and three AVREs, opening a route across the marsh near its widest point. This allowed B Company, arriving at 0745 hours, to push forward to the German positions on the Meuvaines ridge. Owing to the effects of the bombardment, little opposition was encountered (it appears that many of 3/Ost 441's personnel had fled), and the company was able to clear a number of positions towards Meuvaines. Meanwhile, 6th Green Howards' D Company gathered on the shoreline before launching a frontal attack up the slopes to the Mont Fleury battery. Here, owing in part to an act of considerable gallantry by Company Sergeant-Major Stan Hollis (for which he was later awarded the Victoria Cross), German resistance was also mopped up in relatively short order and with minimal casualties.

A few hundred metres to the east, 5th East Yorks' assault also began well. Disembarking without loss on King Red, the Yorkshires' A Company and assault engineers soon created gaps through the coastal minefield and attacked WN-34. This position was covered with bomb and rocket craters, indicating the intensity of the preliminary bombardment. Few of the garrison were in any condition to resist (the muzzle covers had not even been removed from their 50-mm and 75-mm guns) and, after desultory fighting around 30 prisoners were taken. Having suffered only eight casualties, A Company consolidated in preparation for its move inland. While it did so, B Company passed through its position and began clearing Ver-sur-Mer.

The attack on WN-33, however, proved to be a different matter. Although no casualties were sustained during the run-in, when Z Breaching Squadron disembarked west of la Rivière, its vehicles came under point-blank fire from the 88-mm gun at the western end of the sea wall. Two AVREs were hit and exploded, causing numerous casualties among 280th Field Company and the leading infantry of 5th East Yorks' D Company. Meanwhile, machine guns mounted in the seafront villas raked the beach and mortar bombs dropped on the sand. Two of D Company's platoon officers were killed, while the company commander (Captain W. Sugarman) was wounded on reaching the

Initially, 5th East Yorks' clearance of la Rivière was frustrated by high stone walls like this one, at the western end of the Avenue St-Gerbold. Once tank support arrived, the task of mopping up WN-33 proved more straightforward. *(Author)*

US LCI(L)s,
carrying the
three battalions
of 151st Brigade,
approach Gold
Beach, barely
visible through
the smoke in
the background.
A Hunt class
destroyer can be
seen above the
LCI(L)s in the
centre. *(IWM
A23894)*

sea wall. Similar heavy losses (including its commander wounded and second-in-command killed) were suffered by C Company when it arrived to reinforce the attack shortly afterwards. Less than 30 minutes after landing, the survivors of C and D Companies found themselves huddled within a few metres of the enemy beneath the 3-metre sea wall at the top of King Red beach.

Faced with the unravelling of their plan, the British commanders responded with speed and aggression. On the orders of the Deputy Senior Officer, Assault Group King Red, who was observing from *LCH 275*, three Landing Craft Gun (Large) [LCG(L)s] and two other support craft closed to within 1 km of la Rivière, hammering 7/GR 736's positions with 4.7-inch, 6-pounder and automatic cannon fire. Meanwhile, armoured vehicles from the breaching teams and 4th/7th RDG attacked WN-33 from the west. One of them, a Sherman Crab commanded by Captain Roger Bell, succeeded in putting several rounds through the embrasure of the 88-mm gun casemate, knocking it out. With the Germans' fire faltering, 5th East Yorks' commander, Lt-Col G.W. White, then led some of his men over the sea wall and into WN-33, where they started clearing the defenders from their positions.

The ensuing fight for la Rivière was difficult and costly. Although heavily outgunned, *Hauptmann* (Captain)

Gustav-Adolf Lutz's men resisted stubbornly, retreating house by house through the shattered remnants of the village. As they did so, they inflicted further losses on the Yorkshires, as well as killing two of 4th/7th RDG's tank commanders. However, they had no answer to the firepower of the AVREs, at least two of which entered la Rivière in support of the infantry, or to the DD Shermans, which smashed their way through the high stone walls that separated the villa gardens. Soon after 1100 hours, some 40 survivors of 7/GR 736 surrendered. Although more were rounded up later, especially by 2nd Battalion, The Hertfordshire Regiment (the King sector beach security battalion), their capitulation marked the effective end of resistance at the eastern end of Gold Beach.

By late morning 69th Brigade had achieved all its first phase objectives. Having secured the Meuvaines ridge, at approximately 1130 hours 6th Green Howards resumed its attack south. Most of the battalion advanced towards Crépon, although C Company, supported by some DD tanks, headed south-west to clear a suspected rocket projector site (actually II/AR 1716's command post) near the Château de Maromme. Simultaneously, the brigade's reserve battalion, 7th Green Howards, passed through Ver-sur-Mer towards its first target, WN-32. As in the case of WN-34, this position had been struck heavily by the bombardment, and its garrison of 50 or so artillerymen showed no desire to fight. After a few 75-mm rounds from two Churchill Crocodiles accompanying 7th Green Howards, they surrendered. For its part, 5th East Yorks spent the remainder of the morning re-organising at la Rivière and Mont Fleury, forming a composite company from the remnants of C and D Companies, while preparing to follow the rest of 69th Brigade south. Meanwhile, other units consolidated near the beach or joined the advance. These included 86th Field Regiment (plus some late-arriving Royal Marine Centaurs), as well as elements of 102nd Anti-Tank Regiment and 69th Brigade's headquarters, which moved inland at 1130 hours. They were joined by the three battalions of 151st Brigade, which landed in heavy surf on

King sector between 1030 and 1200 hours, before moving to their assembly area west of Ver. Part of 50th Division's headquarters also came ashore, including Maj-Gen Graham, who landed just before midday.

After appearing briefly to hang in the balance, by noon 50th Division's assault had broken the back of the German resistance on Gold Beach. Faced with heavy attacks all along its 35-km front, 716th Division had, for the most part, fought bravely against British and Canadian forces landing on Coast Defence Sector 'Caen'. However, its casualties were considerable, and at Ver-sur-Mer the collapse of most of 441st *Ost* Battalion had played a major part in ensuring the loss of all the division's *Widerstandsnester* in this particular area. Furthermore, despite determined opposition from 352nd Division at le Hamel, 231st Brigade had succeeded in isolating WN-37 and WN-38, and in driving its own spearheads over 2 km inland. Nevertheless, the fact remained that 50th Division's attack was already at least two hours behind schedule. The issue to be decided during the rest of 6 June, therefore, was whether the British could develop sufficient momentum to seize all their D-Day objectives, and in the process expedite XXX Corps' overall plan, or whether the Germans might yet recover from their initial setbacks, and drive their opponents back into the sea.

CHAPTER 4

THE ADVANCE INLAND

For the German high command, the airborne and amphibious landings that began on the morning of 6 June came as a great shock. Despite some warning signs at the start of the month – notably intercepted messages to French resistance groups to prepare for sabotage operations – there was no convincing evidence of an imminent invasion. Owing to the inclement weather, assumptions about the conditions in which an attack would occur did not appear to be fulfilled, and no German vessels were at sea to detect the Allied armada as it entered the Bay of the Seine. Most Germans also continued to believe that any major assault would take place north of Le Havre, and tide and moon tables suggested that an attack in this area was unlikely before 20 June. Consequently, not only were no special counter-measures in place when the first Allied troops landed in Lower Normandy, but several senior German commanders were also absent from their headquarters. Among them was Field Marshal Rommel, who went on leave to Germany on 4 June, and who spent the night of 5–6 June sleeping peacefully at his family home in Herrlingen.

The initial German reaction to Operation Neptune, therefore, was characterised at the highest levels by confusion and disagreement about Allied intentions, and a reluctance to act decisively. For the troops on the ground, however, procrastination was less of an option. By 0115 hours both 352nd and 716th Divisions were on maximum alert; an hour later, so was the rest of LXXXIV Corps. Soon afterwards, the first piecemeal counter-attacks were launched against British airborne

troops east of the River Orne. Despite Army Group B's refusal to place it under Seventh Army's command, elements of 21st Panzer Division also began moving north to reinforce these efforts. Although this heralded significant difficulties for Crocker's I Corps, it also meant that 50th Division would not be exposed to armoured counter-attacks on D-Day. In effect, several hours before the amphibious assault even began, one of Maj-Gen Graham's main concerns – that the enemy's strongest forces in Lower Normandy would strike towards Bayeux instead of Caen – was rendered groundless.

In the absence of reinforcement from the east, the Germans' best chance of halting 50th Division lay in the tactical reserves deployed near Gold Beach itself. These included II/GR 726, whose 700 lightly-armed men were billeted near Crépon, plus a company of eight 88-mm anti-tank guns from 21st Panzer Division, located around St-Léger (two more companies were behind Juno Beach). More significantly, stretching in an arc from St-Gabriel (7 km south of Asnelles) to St-Paul-du-Vernay (10 km south of Bayeux) were the 2,700 soldiers of Battle Group *Meyer*. Equipped with three self-propelled anti-tank guns, 42 artillery pieces and mortars, and almost 170 machine guns, this reinforced regiment was the equal of any of 50th Division's infantry brigades. It had also rehearsed counter-attacks in the direction of Ver-sur-Mer. If it acted as intended, delivering a concentrated blow against the beachhead early on D-Day, it was possible that Graham's troops would be forced onto the defensive. Indeed, since

Allied intelligence had failed completely to identify the battlegroup's presence, the psychological impact of such a counter-attack might have been considerable.

Unfortunately for the Germans, Battle Group *Meyer* proved unable to fulfil its intended role on the morning of 6 June. Just as Montgomery had hoped, the airborne landings that preceded the amphibious assault caused consternation among the defenders. The strong winds that scattered the parachute drops only exacerbated this effect, since it made it difficult to identify points of main effort. When elements of US 101st Airborne Division descended south and east of Carentan, rather than north of it as planned, LXXXIV Corps did not spend time pondering the meaning of their arrival. Instead, interpreting the drops as part of a deliberate attempt to isolate the Cotentin peninsula, it reacted immediately, ordering Battle Group *Meyer* to move from its billeting area towards the Vire estuary. By 0530 hours the battle group was well on its way, travelling by bicycle and truck in widely dispersed groups in the direction of 352nd Division's left flank. As a result, it was in no position to intervene when the first elements of 50th Division landed on Gold Beach two hours later.

Throughout the morning of D-Day, therefore, the German troops between Arromanches and la Rivière received almost no reinforcement. Admittedly, it was not long before LXXXIV Corps recognised its error and tried to correct it. However, although it instructed Battle Group *Meyer* to turn back and begin a counter-attack towards Crépon, it took several hours for the order to reach all the units concerned. Furthermore, although 10 assault guns (*Sturmgeschütze*) from 352nd Division's anti-tank battalion were allocated to support the attack, this barely compensated for the detachment of one of the battlegroup's three infantry battalions, which was sent to assist the attempt to repulse US V Corps' landing on Omaha Beach. By the time the leading elements of Battle Group *Meyer* returned to the area east of Bayeux in the early afternoon, their soldiers were tired and hungry. Having been delayed by Allied fighter-bombers *en route*, they must also have

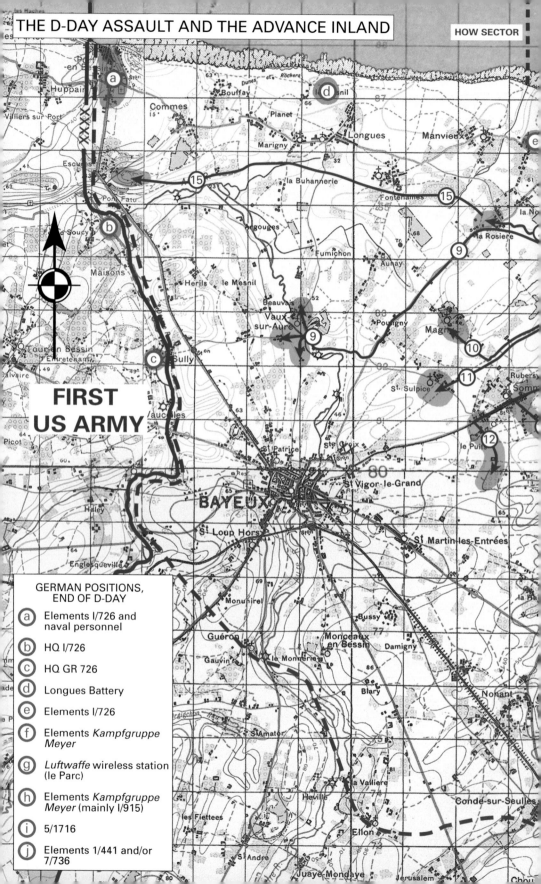

THE D-DAY ASSAULT AND THE ADVANCE INLAND

FIRST US ARMY

GERMAN POSITIONS, END OF D-DAY

(a) Elements I/726 and naval personnel

(b) HQ I/726

(c) HQ GR 726

(d) Longues Battery

(e) Elements I/726

(f) Elements *Kampfgruppe Meyer*

(g) *Luftwaffe* wireless station (le Parc)

(h) Elements *Kampfgruppe Meyer* (mainly I/915)

(i) 5/1716

(j) Elements 1/441 and/or 7/736

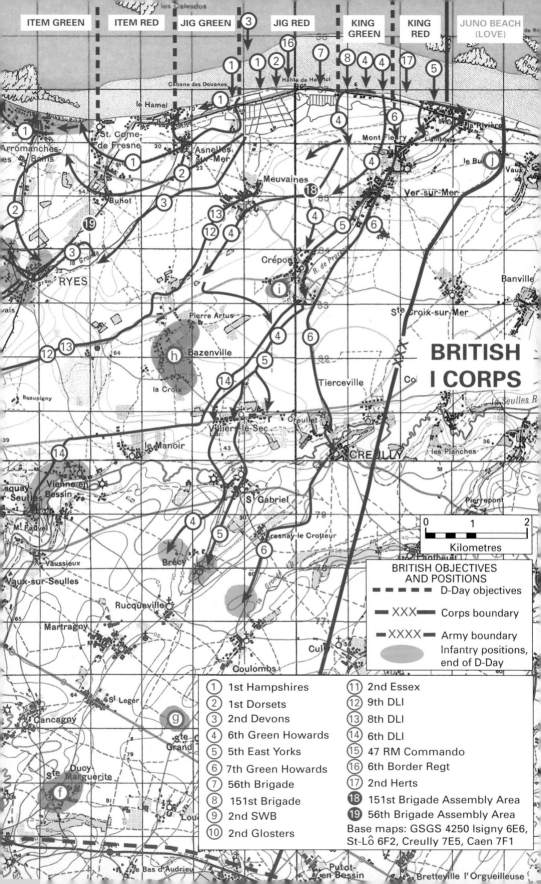

BRITISH
I CORPS

ITEM GREEN   ITEM RED   JIG GREEN   JIG RED   KING GREEN   KING RED   JUNO BEACH (LOVE)

le Hamel
Cabane des Douanes
Hâble de Heurtot
St. Côme-de-Fresne
Asnelles-sur-Mer
Arromanches-les-Bains
Buhot
Meuvaines
Mont Fleury
Ver-sur-Mer
la Rivière
Limbourg
le Bu
Vaux
RYES
la Gronde
Crépon
R. de Provence
Banville
Pierre Artus
Bazenville
la Croix
Ste Croix-sur-Mer
Tierceville
Beaupigny
Creullet
Villiers-le-Sec
le Manoir
S'. Gabriel
CREULLY
les Planches
Pierrepont
Vienne-en-Bessin
M'. Fauvel
Vaussieux
Brécy
la Gronde
Vaux-sur-Seulles
Rucqueville
Martragny
Fresnay-le-Crotteur
Coulombs
Culy
Cancagny
St Léger
Ste Grand
Ste Duoy Marguerite
Loud
Je Bas d'Audrieu
Putot-en-Bessin
Bretteville l'Orgueilleuse

Kilometres
0   1   2

BRITISH OBJECTIVES
AND POSITIONS

- - - - -   D-Day objectives
━XXX━   Corps boundary
━XXXX━   Army boundary
▓▓▓   Infantry positions,
       end of D-Day

① 1st Hampshires   ⑪ 2nd Essex
② 1st Dorsets   ⑫ 9th DLI
③ 2nd Devons   ⑬ 8th DLI
④ 6th Green Howards   ⑭ 6th DLI
⑤ 5th East Yorks   ⑮ 47 RM Commando
⑥ 7th Green Howards   ⑯ 6th Border Regt
⑦ 56th Brigade   ⑰ 2nd Herts
⑧ 151st Brigade   ⑱ 151st Brigade Assembly Area
⑨ 2nd SWB   ⑲ 56th Brigade Assembly Area
⑩ 2nd Glosters   Base maps: GSGS 4250 Isigny 6E6,
                       St-Lô 6F2, Creully 7E5, Caen 7F1

wondered whether the moment for a successful counter-attack had not in fact already passed.

While the Germans struggled to recover their equilibrium, 69th Brigade continued to make steady progress on 50th Division's left flank. With most of II/GR 726 drawn into a desperate battle against the Canadians near Ste-Croix-sur-Mer, 3 km from Juno Beach, the brigade faced no significant resistance. Although scattered parties of defenders, including elements of 441st *Ost* Battalion and some of II/AR 1716's artillerymen, did what they could to delay the advance, by 1300 hours the first British troops (probably from 7th Green Howards) had entered Crépon. Others, including 4th/7th RDG's A Squadron and most of 6th and 7th Green Howards, by-passed the village on its eastern side. Meanwhile, some 2 km west of Crépon, 6th Green Howards' C Company and 4th/7th RDG's B Squadron attacked the suspected rocket projector site (WN-35b) in a small wood near the Château de Maromme. After a brief fight, during which the defenders' ammunition store exploded and 12 Germans were killed, 40 prisoners (including a lieutenant-colonel) were taken. The British lost one man wounded.

The Mont Fleury lighthouse, damaged by the bombardment. The building still exists, but it is closed to the public. *(Dupont collection)*

Leaving behind several pockets of resistance, 69th Brigade pressed on across open country towards its second phase objectives, which lay north and south of the River Seulles. On the western axis, which ran along the track from Crépon to Villiers-le-Sec (code-named 'Rubicon Road'), the advance was spearheaded by 5th East Yorks. It was followed closely by 6th Green Howards and supported by 86th Field Regiment, which took up firing positions south-west of Crépon, and by some of 2nd Cheshires' machine guns. 7th Green Howards' D Company, 4th/7th RDG's B Squadron and 102nd Anti-Tank Regiment's 99th Battery also moved

along this route. Further east, on 'Hudson Highway' (the modern D65), 7th Green Howards overcame a group of Germans 500 metres beyond Crépon, taking another 40 prisoners. The battalion then advanced towards the small town of Creully, crossing the road from Villiers-le-Sec to Tierceville at about 1500 hours. In accordance with the operation order, the attack was led by a mobile column consisting of a section of the Green Howards' own carriers and 17 DD tanks from 4th/7th RDG's A Squadron, carrying 7th Green Howards' B Company on their hulls. The unit was led by 7th Green Howards' acting deputy battalion commander, Major H.E. Bowley.

On reaching the Seulles valley, Bowley was pleasantly surprised to discover that neither of the bridges over the river (which divides into two branches as it passes Creully) had been demolished. However, as the first of A Squadron's Shermans approached from the north, it was fired at by a German self-propelled gun stationed near the entrance to the town. Fearing the loss of momentum if his vehicles became involved in street fighting in Creully, 7th Green Howards' commander, Lt-Col P.H. Richardson, withdrew the mobile column and sent it to reconnoitre possible crossing sites further west. In the meantime, he ordered C Company (Major Don Warrener) to capture the town. Following a preliminary bombardment by some of 86th Field Regiment's 25-pounders, arranged by the attached forward observation officer, the company attacked. There was no opposition, and Warrener's men advanced up the winding road into the centre of Creully, where they came under fire from the eastern end of the high street. It was rapidly established that

This panorama shows King Green and Jig Red sectors, with numerous villages and roads, as far as St-Gabriel and Lantheuil, visible inland. (IWM MH24333)

their adversaries were Canadians from the Royal Winnipeg Rifles, who had landed on Juno Beach earlier that morning. Once contact was made and the shooting stopped, the town was secured with little difficulty. The mobile column – which had reached Villiers-le-Sec without discovering another road bridge – then retraced its steps and passed through Creully into the fields south-west of the town. The rest of 7th Green Howards (less D Company, which continued along Rubicon Road) followed. The time was approximately 1800 hours.

Further west, 5th East Yorks and 6th Green Howards, plus their supporting armour, also pushed forward, approaching Villiers-le-Sec during the mid-afternoon. As they did so, they encountered elements of Battle Group *Meyer*, which began moving into its counter-attack positions at about 1600 hours. Particularly strong resistance came from 352nd Fusilier Battalion, which entered Villiers-le-Sec at much the same time as 69th Brigade launched its assault. After a sharp fight, during which 5th East Yorks' CO was wounded, the village was taken by flank attacks by 6th Green Howards' B and D Companies (assisted by 7th Green Howards' mobile column), and the British continued their advance. 352nd Fusilier Battalion withdrew before them, making a determined stand at St-Gabriel, on the south bank of the Seulles, before being forced back towards Brécy. It was supported by 352nd Division's assault guns, which began arriving from the south at about 1800 hours. However, although the Germans destroyed six of 4th/7th

RDG's Shermans (two from B Squadron, and four from A Squadron near Fresnay le Crotteur), they lost four of their own *Sturmgeschütze*. The assault gun detachment's commander, *Oberleutnant* (Lieutenant) Dzialas was killed, as was the CO of the fusilier battalion, *Hauptmann* (Captain) Gerth. When *Hauptmann* Hertzfeld, Gerth's successor, was captured along with many of his men at St-Gabriel, German resistance began to crumble. Although the survivors rallied in the orchards around Brécy, when 6th Green Howards and 5th East Yorks launched a set-piece attack with artillery and machine gun support at about 2100 hours, the defenders had already retreated. According to 352nd Division's telephone log, by the time it reached Ducy-Ste-Marguerite (5 km south-west of Brécy) later that evening, 352nd Fusilier Battalion had only 40 of its original 700 personnel left under command.

Battle Group *Meyer*'s intervention failed completely in its aim of driving the British back into the sea. Nevertheless, it did impose delays on 69th Brigade, which might otherwise have reached its D-Day objectives. Furthermore, an aerial reconnaissance report that 40 armoured vehicles (presumably the battle group's *Sturmgeschütze*, exaggerated four-fold) were advancing north from Rucqueville caused some disquiet when it was received at Maj-Gen Graham's headquarters at 1820 hours. With few armoured reserves available, 50th Division was compelled to send 11 Sherman Crabs to take up defensive

The view from Asnelles towards Buhot. 1st Dorsets advanced around midday from the left hand edge of the photo to seize Point 54, which is visible above the houses of le Carrefour. Later, part of the battalion attacked through the woodland on the skyline to capture WN-40, on the high ground at the extreme right of the photo. *(Author)*

positions south of Creully. Even worse, owing to mis-identification by a newly arrived artillery spotting aircraft, at 1940 hours HMS *Orion* opened fire with its 6-inch guns on 4th/7th RDG's A Squadron about 1,500 metres east of Brécy. No vehicles were destroyed, but casualties were caused both to tank crews and the accompanying infantry. Thanks to prompt action by 86th Field Regiment's forward observation officer (Captain Perry), who reported the mistake by radio, HMS *Orion*'s fire was stopped at 2012. 7th Green Howards then made good progress, reaching Coulombs around 2100 hours. However, when struck by rocket, artillery and machine-gun fire from a fortified radio station (le Parc) near the N13 highway, its advance came to a halt. In view of the battalion's isolated position (the Canadians on its left and the rest of 69th Brigade were several kilometres behind), it was decided to withdraw 7th Green Howards to spend the night on the high ground east of Rucqueville. Similarly, having captured Brécy, 6th Green Howards and 5th East Yorks were instructed to consolidate their positions around the village and prepare to resume their advance the following morning.

At the opposite end of 50th Division's beachhead, 231st Brigade also had to work hard to break German resistance during the afternoon of D-Day. Some of the heaviest fighting took place at le Hamel, where 1st Hampshires struggled for several hours to neutralise the two seafront *Widerstandsnester*. As recounted in Tour B (*pp. 132–49*), not until 1700 hours was Asnelles cleared and WN-37 finally subdued. Fortunately, once the latter position had fallen, it proved relatively straightforward to capture WN-38. By early evening, engineers were making excellent progress in removing obstacles from Jig sector (low tide was at 1746 hours) and in improving the exits through the minefield at the top of the beach. In an effort to clear the considerable backlog of traffic on the western part of Gold Beach, repairs also continued on the coastal road, and to the routes inland.

Less than 2 km from Asnelles, at the foot of the slopes overlooking Jig sector, 1st Dorsets' leading companies (C and D) reached le Buhot around midday. Pushing through the hamlet to Point 54 (near Point 56 on modern maps), C Company was fired upon by German troops on the hilltop, and withdrew. A second attempt, using cover provided by hedges and ditches, proved more successful, and after killing seven Germans and capturing 17, the Dorsets took possession of the feature. Simultaneously, while moving south along the road to Ryes, D Company surprised a group of German pioneers (probably from 59th Engineer Construction Battalion, which had several hundred men in the area) and took them prisoner. D Company then moved onto Point 54, where it joined battalion headquarters and C Company in preparing to attack the *Widerstandsnest* 500 metres to the north (WN-40). Meanwhile, to secure the Dorsets' gains against counter-attacks, several anti-tank guns were deployed at le Carrefour crossroads (marked on 1944 maps as St-Côme-de-Fresne), a short distance away.

According to its war diary, 1st Dorsets' attack on WN-40 began at 1500 hours (other sources place the attack over an hour earlier). The assault was supported by 90th Field Regiment from its battery positions near Meuvaines and by the Vickers machine guns of 2nd Cheshires' 11 Platoon, firing from Point 54. Help was also provided by approximately eight tanks from the Sherwood Rangers' C Squadron. Initial progress was good, and after some close-quarters fighting the Dorsets' D Company (Major W.N. Hayes) overran several heavy weapons in a wood 250 metres south of the main defences. However, weakened by its casualties, D Company was unable to make further progress. The Dorsets' CO, Lt-Col E.A.M. Norie, therefore decided to bring forward his reserve (A Company) to renew the attack. After another artillery bombardment, and covered by fire from C and D Companies, A Company (Captain R. Royle) advanced across the open ground south-west of WN-40. Using the protection provided by the numerous shell holes surrounding the site, its soldiers broke through the wire perimeter and began clearing the defenders from their trenches and bunkers. Overwhelmed by the all-arms assault to which they had been subjected, most of the garrison surrendered quickly, although a few

La Gronde Ruisseau. The photo is taken from the D65, looking south-west. It was along this stream that 2nd Devons advanced towards its objective. *(Author)*

fought to the death. Around 40 prisoners, among them artillery observers, were taken.

While 1st Dorsets fought to establish a presence on the high ground west of Asnelles, 231st Brigade's reserve battalion, 2nd Devons, encountered equally tough opposition as it pushed up the broad valley of la Gronde Ruisseau. Some of this came from mortars and artillery located to the south. Despite the death of their commander, *Rittmeister* (Captain) Schleich, I/GR 916's infantry also resisted stubbornly, and even attempted to counter-attack the British troops as they advanced. These efforts were broken up, but when the Devons' leading companies (A and D) reached a thickly hedged area in the valley bottom 1 km north-east of Ryes, their assault stalled under intense close range fire. Had artillery support been available, the enemy could probably have been overcome fairly quickly. However, 90th and 147th Field Regiments were busy assisting other units, 2nd Devons' own mortar platoon was not yet deployed and the attached FOB (Captain Dupont, with a radio link to the destroyer HMS *Jervis*) was forbidden to call down fire within 1,000 yards (915 metres) of his own troops. After some costly attempts to break through, by mid-afternoon 2nd Devons found itself stuck and unable to reach its objective.

Lt-Col Nevill was aware of the importance of capturing Ryes, which lay astride one of 50th Division's main axes of advance, as rapidly as possible. Consequently, at about 1530 hours he ordered A Company to remain in the valley to fix the enemy, while B and D Companies outflanked the Germans to the west. The move was successful, and an hour later B Company (assisted by three M10 tank destroyers from 102nd Anti-Tank Regiment) entered Ryes. There was slight opposition from troops of 352nd Division's NCO training school, which had rushed to the area to try to assist I/GR 916, but the Germans soon withdrew. While anti-tank guns deployed to protect the village, elements of 2nd Devons advanced onto the slopes 500 metres north-west of Ryes. Here they took possession of a number of empty dug-outs, including the abandoned headquarters of I/GR 916.

The capture of Ryes represented the end of significant resistance on 50th Division's right flank. Although occasional skirmishes erupted as 231st Brigade moved forward during the rest of D-Day, many of the remaining second phase objectives fell quickly and at little cost. These included *Stützpunkt Arromanches*, WN-43 and WN-44, all of which were taken by 1st Hampshires before 2100 hours. The village of Arromanches itself also fell into the Hampshires' hands, while 1 km to the south 1st Dorsets secured WN-41 (le Petit Fontaine), capturing four 105-mm guns which had been abandoned by their crews. The Dorsets then moved south to relieve 2nd Devons at Ryes, so that the Devons could continue the advance to the west. However, although the Devons' C Company – which had spent most

The valley of la Gronde Ruisseau, looking south-west from the high ground above Meuvaines (in the centre of the photo) towards Ryes. Asnelles is just off the right hand side of the photo. 2nd Devons advanced from right to left to capture Ryes during the afternoon of 6 June. *(Author)*

of the day in le Hamel – managed to reach la Rosière at about 1900 hours, when further resistance was encountered it was decided to consolidate the battalion's positions for the night. Similarly, after infiltrating across country during the evening, 47 RM Commando dug in on the high ground at Point 72, 2 km from the coast. Like 2nd Devons' objective at the Longues Battery, the commando attack on Port-en-Bessin would have to wait for the following day.

Once the assault forces had broken through the coastal defences, the two reserve brigades also started to head inland. The troops of 151st (Durham Light Infantry) Brigade were the first to set off, advancing at 1530 hours from Ver and Meuvaines towards objectives south-east of Bayeux. Although 56th Brigade's departure was delayed by its late landing, and then by congestion between Gold Beach and the assembly area near le Buhot, at 1745 hours it too began moving south. Both brigade groups were reinforced with tanks, machine guns and heavy mortars, and had artillery support from 90th and 147th Field Regiments. As planned, each battalion was led by a mobile column, comprising carrier-mounted heavy weapons, anti-tank guns and an infantry company on bicycles (in addition, 6th DLI was assisted by 4th/7th RDG's C Squadron, and 2nd Essex by the Sherwood Rangers' A Squadron). The role of these units was to seize their brigades' third phase objectives before the enemy could recover. After the main bodies arrived to consolidate, they would then push on to try to capture their final D-Day targets by nightfall.

Although hindered by traffic jams, 151st Brigade made good progress during the late afternoon and evening of D-Day. Advancing in the wake of 69th Brigade, 6th DLI's mobile column reached Villiers-le-Sec at about 1800 hours. Ignoring the battle raging to the south, it then thrust west to the village of Vienne-en-Bessin. Meanwhile, 2 km further north, 9th DLI spearheaded the attack along the main road towards Bayeux, reaching the hamlet of Pierre Solain at 1700 hours and Sommervieu 80 minutes later. Neither of the leading battalions encountered more than sporadic resistance,

and dozens of prisoners were sent to the rear. Reflecting the confused nature of the battle, during its advance 9th DLI's mobile column was mistaken for Germans, and strafed by RAF Typhoons; luckily, no casualties were incurred. Much more unfortunate, however, was the fate that befell Brigadier R.H. Senior of 151st Brigade. Moving forward to visit his troops, at about 1630 hours his jeep was ambushed by a pocket of Germans near Bazenville (from Battle Group *Meyer*'s I/GR 915). Senior's driver and intelligence officer were both killed, and the brigadier himself was wounded and captured. Unsurprisingly, this had a disruptive effect on 151st Brigade's command and control. Although Maj-Gen Graham went to brigade headquarters to provide direction, and an acting commander (Lt-Col R.P. Lidwill, 8th DLI) was appointed, it was decided to halt the brigade's advance until the situation was clarified. As a result, 6th DLI was ordered to dig in at Esquay-sur-Seulles, while 9th DLI did the same around Caugy farm (la Croix de Caugy on modern maps), 2 km to the north-west. 8th DLI and brigade headquarters also took up defensive positions in and around Sommervieu.

North of the Durhams, 56th Brigade finally struck out through Ryes at about 1800 hours. Moving west

Although posed, this neatly illustrates British equipment in 1944. A Sten gun can be seen in the foreground. The men are from 151st Brigade. *(IWM B5378)*

50TH (NORTHUMBRIAN) DIVISION, D-DAY CASUALTIES

Unit	Killed	Wounded	Missing
Jig Sector Assault Troops			
1st Hampshires	64	118	–
1st Dorsets	21	98	9
2nd Devons	22	66	some
82nd Assault Squadron, RE	2	5	–
B Squadron, Westminster Dragoons	–	4	2
73rd Field Company, RE	4	10	12
295th Field Company, RE	5	10	–
LCOCU 9 and 10	casualties described as 'heavy'		
Sherwood Rangers Yeomanry	9	15	–
1st RM Armoured Support Regt	–	at least 6	–
15 Troop, C Squadron, 141st RAC	1	–	1
King Sector Assault Troops			
5th East Yorks	28	approx. 70	–
6th Green Howards	18	approx. 65	–
7th Green Howards	10	approx. 30	–
C Squadron, Westminster Dragoons	–	–	–
81st Assault Squadron, RE	1	12	5
280th Field Company, RE	8	26	–
233rd Field Company, RE	7	10	1
LCOCUs 3 & 4	1	4	–
4th/7th Royal Dragoon Guards	12	18	–
1st RM Armoured Support Regt	–	–	–
13 Troop, C Squadron, 141st RAC	–	–	–
Other Units			
6th Durham Light Infantry	–	–	–
8th Durham Light Infantry	–	2	–
9th Durham Light Infantry	possibly 2	–	–
2nd Glosters	–	5	–
2nd Essex	–	4	–
2nd South Wales Borderers	at least 2	at least 2	–
86th Field Regt, RA	3	at least 3	1

from Ryes, 2nd SWB quickly reached la Rosière, where it passed through 2nd Devons' outposts. It then continued towards its objectives, which lay on the high ground between the River Aure and the River Drôme north of Bayeux. The Borderers met resistance at a radio station near Pouligny (WN-46), but after an attack by their D Company the Germans retreated. The forward body then pressed on through close country to the bridge at Vaux-sur-Aure, securing it just before midnight. Meanwhile, 2nd Essex

Unit	Killed	Wounded	Missing
90th Field Regt, RA	6	3	–
147th Field Regt, RA	1	at least 2	–
102nd Anti-Tank Regt, RA	–	3	–
61st Recce Regt	up to 25 killed and wounded		
2nd Cheshires	at least 1	at least 7	–
47 RM Commando	29	32	–
2nd Hertfordshires	4	–	–
6th Border Regt	–	–	–
24th Lancers	–	–	–

Total casualties for Allied land, sea and air forces directly involved in the assault on Gold Beach on 6 June were 1,000–1,100 men. Around 350 were killed. Some of the figures in the table are estimates, given the differences between sources. Brigadier Senior was wounded and captured on 6 June (but subsequently escaped); 2 members of his staff were killed. No detailed information is available for the divisional support units, but their overall casualties were probably low (divisional signals lost 1 killed, 5 wounded). Naval losses are unavailable, probably totalling 20 fatalities and more wounded. RAF and USAAF casualties are also unavailable; several bombers were lost, with up to 60 dead. There were no French civilian fatalities in Asnelles, Meuvaines or Crépon, but 13 citizens of Ver-sur-Mer were killed during the fighting or by the preliminary bombardment. German casualty figures are unavailable; at least 1,000 prisoners were taken (including some wounded).

Memorial in Bayeux to the Essex Regiment. *(Author)*

advanced against little opposition to the St-Sulpice crossroads. Although some of the attached Sherwood Rangers tanks continued to the outskirts of Bayeux, by the time they got there it was dusk. Since it was unclear how strongly Bayeux was held, it was decided to consolidate the positions already gained. 2nd Glosters therefore moved with brigade HQ to Magny-en-Bessin, arriving at 0026 hours on 7 June. Some 3 km further west, 2nd SWB's main body also advanced to Vaux-sur-Aure, where it spent much of the night patrolling, rounding up stray Germans and preparing to defend the bridge against counter-attacks.

At the end of 6 June, 50th Division remained about 6 km short of its D-Day objectives. To the west, there seemed no prospect of an imminent link-up with US V Corps, which had struggled all day to gain a foothold on Omaha Beach, 15 km away. Owing to the bad weather and damage sustained by Force G's landing craft (34 LCTs were lost or disabled), the build-up of men and matériel on Gold Beach was also behind schedule. 7th Armoured Division, which planned to disembark most of its armoured brigade during the evening, was able to land only a few tanks. Several of 50th Division's units were in a similar situation. Most significantly, they included 24th Lancers and 61st Recce Regiment, both of which had been allocated an important role in spearheading XXX Corps' advance south. Their absence, combined with 50th Division's inability to reach its D-Day objectives, effectively ruled out any chance of a thrust to Villers-Bocage on the night of 6–7 June. Potentially, this represented a major blow to Second Army's intentions and Montgomery's overall plan.

The destroyer HMS *Beagle* brings Lt-Gen Bucknall to Gold Beach during the evening of 6 June; la Rivière is in the background. Bucknall boarded HMS *Bulolo* at about 1830 hours, before going ashore and spending the night at 50th Division's headquarters in Meuvaines. *(IWM A23872)*

Nevertheless, Maj-Gen Graham had reason to be pleased with his division's achievement. Through the combined efforts of the air, sea and land forces, the worst effects of the weather and enemy resistance had been overcome. A beachhead of over 70 square kilometres had been created and a firm connection established with Canadian 3rd Infantry Division, which had made good

progress inland from Juno Beach. The logistics organisation (104 Beach Sub-Area) was taking shape and, thanks partly to its hard work, around 20,000 men were already safely ashore, together with 2,100 vehicles and about 1,000 tons of supplies. All of this had also been achieved at much smaller cost than had been feared before the assault. Instead of the 1,795 wounded anticipated by the planners, 50th Division had suffered fewer than 700. Although casualties in several units had been severe, not one of Maj-Gen Graham's battalions had been rendered combat-ineffective. Unlike the troops opposing them, all would be capable of acting offensively the following day.

For the Germans, D-Day had been a catastrophe. Nowhere along the Lower Normandy coast had they succeeded in halting the Allied onslaught. In the Gold Beach area, all their major units had been badly mauled or – in the case of 441st *Ost* Battalion and II/AR 1716 – destroyed. Although an order issued by 352nd Division at 2233 hours to establish a new front along the line Brécy–Esquay-sur-Seulles–Sommervieu–Pouligny–Tracy-sur-Mer seemed sensible enough, it was almost meaningless, not least because only one of these places (the last) was actually in German hands. Despite promises of reinforcement, nor was it reasonable to assume that any ground could be retaken the following day. Nevertheless, by nightfall the German high command had at least decided to commit some of its armoured divisions. In particular, I SS Panzer Corps had been released from the OKW reserve, with the task of counter-attacking Second Army's beachhead between Bayeux and the River Orne. Subordinated to it would be two of the most powerful formations available to the *Wehrmacht*, namely 12th SS Panzer Division and the Panzer Lehr Division. Although there was little prospect of their complete arrival before 8 June, 50th Division would need to make the most of its opportunity on D+1 to develop its offensive. If it did not do so, even assuming it gained its original objectives, it could still face considerable difficulties in the days ahead.

CHAPTER 5

CONSOLIDATION

For most of 50th Division's soldiers, the night of 6–7 June was a sleepless one, spent either digging in or patrolling. Since hundreds of Germans had been by-passed during the assault, there were several clashes before dawn. After a day during which the *Luftwaffe* had been almost entirely absent from the Normandy skies, from dusk on 6 June small groups of German aircraft also began to appear over the Gold Beach area. Some were shot down before they could strike at the mass of targets below, but others bombed the beachhead or raided shipping offshore. Little damage resulted, although a few casualties were caused in le Hamel and a road was temporarily blocked in Ver-sur-Mer. The most significant attack occurred shortly after 0600 hours, when HMS *Bulolo* was hit by a 250-lb phosphorus bomb dropped by a Focke-Wulf Fw 190 fighter-bomber. However, although the vessel's operations room was holed and many records destroyed, the ship remained on station. In any case, with 50th Division's headquarters already established in Meuvaines, even minor German successes of this kind were too little and too late.

Soon after 0500 hours on 7 June, the British advance resumed. Opposition was almost non-existent, especially around Bayeux. Here, 151st Brigade's mobile columns reached their objectives between the River Aure and the River Seulles by 0815. Within an hour they were reinforced by their main bodies, plus their accompanying anti-tank

Major L.S. Clayton (*right*), commander of 280th Field Company, RE, examines a steel tetrahedron ('Czech hedgehog') on the beach at la Rivière. The obstacle still has an anti-tank mine attached. *(IWM A23991)*

SECURING THE RIGHT FLANK, 7–8 JUNE

ALLIED MOVEMENTS AND POSITIONS

1. 47 RM Commando, 7 June
2. 1st Hampshires, 7 June
3. 2nd Devons, 7 June
4. 2nd SWB, 7 June
5. 2nd Glosters, 7 June
6. 2nd Essex, 7 June
7. 9th DLI, 7 June
8. 6th DLI, 7 June
9. 3/16th US Inf Regt, 7 June
10. 2nd Devons, 8 June
11. 2nd SWB, 8 June
12. 1/26th US Inf Regt, 8 June
13. 3/26th US Inf Regt, 8 June

XXXX Army boundary

– – – D-Day objectives

British infantry positions, pm 7 June

GERMAN MOVEMENTS AND POSITIONS

9. Patrols, 12th SS Recce Battalion, 7–8 June
15. Elements 30 Mob Bde & GR 726, night 8/9 June
a. Longues Battery (4/1260)
b. Château Maisons (HQ I/726)
c. Château Sully (HQ GR 726)

0 1 2

Kilometres

DD tanks from 4th/7th Royal Dragoon Guards, supporting 69th Brigade, advance near Rucqueville on the morning of 7 June. (IWM MH2327)

and machine-gun units. Eight km south-east of Bayeux, 6th DLI quickly established a front across the road to Tilly-sur-Seulles, blocking the approaches from the south. The battalion also occupied positions along the west side of the Seulles valley, and set up an outpost at the bridge carrying the Bayeux–Caen railway across the river at Condé-sur-Seulles. Further north, 9th DLI dug in on the slopes overlooking the Aure, with 8th DLI in reserve. Contact was also established with 56th Brigade, which entered Bayeux at midday. Reflecting the collapse of German resistance in this sector, few difficulties were encountered in clearing the town, and by early afternoon 2nd Glosters had advanced 1 km south-west of Bayeux. Meanwhile 2nd Essex, supported by the Sherwood Rangers' A Squadron and a troop of AVREs, skirted the eastern edge of Bayeux, overcoming weak opposition near the railway station before crossing the River Aure. After a delay at St-Loup-Hors, where a destroyed bridge obstructed the advance, at about 1800 hours 2nd Essex reached its final objectives on the high ground east of the River Drôme. North of Bayeux, 2nd SWB also moved forward, occupying the orchards around le Gibet (le Parquet on British 1944 maps). From here the battalion was able to dominate the main route north to Port-en-Bessin. However, attempts to establish outposts at Sully and Vaucelles, in anticipation of US V Corps' arrival on the River Drôme, prompted a violent reaction and were abandoned in favour of a stronger attack with armoured support the following day.

Elsewhere, 50th Division made generally satisfactory progress towards its D-Day objectives. On the extreme left flank 7th Green Howards again ran up against opposition when it approached the German radio station south of Coulombs. Owing to the very open country in this area, an attack on this well fortified position was far from straightforward. However, gaps were made in the minefields under cover of a smokescreen, and A and C Companies then attacked from west and east respectively. Support was provided by 4th/7th RDG's A Squadron and the Vickers machine guns of 2nd Cheshires' B Company. After a short battle, which cost the Green Howards seven killed or wounded, the garrison of 50 *Luftwaffe* personnel surrendered. 7th Green Howards then continued south, reaching the N13 west of Ste-Croix-Grand-Tonne around midday. Here it linked up with 5th East Yorks, which had already occupied St-Léger, and established defensive positions on both sides of the highway. In the afternoon, 7th Green Howards also set up a small outpost with the Royal Winnipeg Rifles (from the Juno Beach forces) north of Brouay. Meanwhile, 6th Green Howards advanced to Ducy-Ste-Marguerite, entering the village at about 1100 hours. Pushing forward to the woods overlooking the railway, the battalion came under heavy mortar fire, while snipers also became active. The CO, Lt-Col R.H. Hastings, consulted Brigadier F.Y. Knox and they decided to withdraw and consolidate on the high ground north of Ducy. This was duly done by 1400 hours, although not before 6th Green Howards was attacked both by British and German aircraft, which caused several casualties before the battalion was safely dug in.

At the opposite end of the beachhead, 1st Hampshires and 1st Dorsets spent the first half of 7 June mopping up their second phase objectives, taking around 20 prisoners. 231st Brigade's principal action, however, took place at the Longues Battery. The attack on this position was carried out by elements of 2nd Devons, which advanced from the area around Ryes shortly after dawn. While most of the battalion occupied the heights west of la Rosière, the Devons' C Company headed north, reaching the village of Longues by 0800. Following a short bombardment by naval forces and an air strike by RAF fighter-bombers, the company then attacked the gun position. Resistance from the shell-shocked garrison was sporadic and, although 2nd Devons' mortar officer (Captain P.E. Clark) was shot dead near the clifftop observation post, the battery was overrun by 1100 hours. Having rounded up almost 100 Germans, 2nd Devons then spent the rest of the day securing its front between la Rosière and the coast. Meanwhile, 1st Hampshires went into reserve at Sommervieu, where it was joined during the afternoon by 50th Division's headquarters, which moved forward from Meuvaines to be closer to the new front line.

By the late afternoon of D+1, at the cost of fewer than 100 additional casualties, Maj-Gen Graham's troops had secured almost all their D-Day objectives. Only on the right flank, where some Germans still seemed determined to fight, and where contact was yet to be established with the Americans, did the situation appear uncertain. Nevertheless, during the evening another significant success was recorded when Port-en-Bessin was liberated by 47 RM Commando after a fierce battle (*described in Tour C, pp. 150–68*). By 1800 hours a number of German pockets had also been wiped out behind 50th Division's front lines. The largest of these was around Bazenville, where a substantial portion of Battle Group *Meyer* had been cut off the previous day. Thanks to a co-operative effort by elements of 24th Lancers,

British troops inspect the wreckage of a Messerschmitt Bf 109, shot down near Tilly-sur-Seulles. *(IWM B5461)*

1st Dorsets, 1st Hampshires and 8th DLI, over 200 Germans (mostly from I/GR 915) were killed or captured in this area before nightfall. Brigadier Senior, who had been ambushed near Bazenville on 6 June, also escaped from captivity, although his wounds meant that he had to be evacuated to England. Perhaps more important, various papers carried by the brigadier, including full details of 50th Division's codes for the next fortnight, were also recovered, thus avoiding what might have been a costly security failure.

Despite the lack of resistance to 50th Division's advance on 7 June, German combat power was in fact building up rapidly opposite Second Army's front. This was most evident north-west of Caen, where elements of 12th SS Panzer Division, arriving from east of the River Orne, became involved in heavy fighting against Canadian 3rd Infantry Division. Even in XXX Corps' zone, however, there were signs of increased German strength and resolve. South of the N13, at least two attacks took place against British outposts during the latter part of the day. These were carried out by patrols from 12th SS Reconnaissance Battalion (*SS-Panzeraufklärungsabteilung 12*), which established its command post at Audrieu, 2.5 km south-east of Ducy-Ste-Marguerite. The same unit may also have accounted for two tanks of 4th/7th RDG's C Squadron, which were destroyed while reconnoitring the railway crossing at le Bas d'Audrieu during the afternoon. Despite attempts by the Allied air forces to interdict their movement, by the end of 7 June some very powerful formations were also approaching 50th Division's positions from the south. These included 12th SS Panzer Division's 26th SS Panzergrenadier Regiment, plus most of the Panzer

Jig Green beach, 7 June. Asnelles is just visible at the top. Note how the large expanse of firm sand made the beach well suited to landings like this. *(IWM B500)*

This air photograph, of 28 May 1944, shows most of the area over which 8th Armoured Brigade's battles raged 8–11 June. *(Keele University Air Photo Archive)*

Key

a. Bucéels
b. le Pont Roch
c. Ducy-Ste-Marguerite
d. Tilly-sur-Seulles
e. St-Pierre
f. Point 103
g. Château d'Audrieu

h. Audrieu
i. les Hauts Vents
j. Cristot
k. Parc des Bois Londe
l. Fontenay-le-Pesnel
m. Point 102
n. Bayeux–Caen railway

Lehr Division's mechanised infantry. According to a I SS Panzer Corps order, these troops were to attack towards the coast on 8 June. They would be supported by the Panzer Lehr's tank, engineer and anti-tank battalions, which were to assemble south-east of Tilly-sur-Seulles, and by the division's reconnaissance battalion, providing flank protection east of the River Aure.

The implications of I SS Panzer Corps' arrival became clearer on D+2, when it launched spasmodic attacks against Canadian 7th Infantry Brigade, occupying positions to the east of 50th Division. The Germans' efforts were badly co-ordinated and, owing to the disruption caused by Allied air power, lacked punch. Most of the fighting was done by 26th SS Panzergrenadier Regiment. Although it drove the Royal Winnipeg Rifles from Putot-en-Bessin, Canadian counter-attacks soon regained most of the lost ground. Nevertheless, owing to the arrival of part of the Panzer Lehr's 902nd Panzergrenadier Regiment, by nightfall there were at least 4,000 heavily-armed Germans south of the Bayeux–Caen railway between Audrieu and Norrey-en-Bessin. Combined with the presence of 12th SS Reconnaissance Battalion and strong elements of the Panzer Lehr Division approaching the front to the west, this represented a formidable obstacle to British attempts to advance inland. Furthermore, although most of Second Army's attacks up to now had occurred over open ground, the countryside south of the N13 (and even more so west of the River Seulles) was characterised by dense patches of *bocage*. These consisted of numerous small fields, orchards and copses, bordered by earth banks and high, thick hedges with narrow sunken lanes between them. As well as channelling advances along predictable routes, the *bocage* dramatically reduced visibility, providing cover for defenders while lessening the effectiveness of the attackers' firepower and hampering all-arms co-operation. In short, it represented a superb defensive environment which the German troops now entering the area were well able to exploit.

A 24th Lancers' Sherman Firefly (identifiable by its long-barrelled 17-pounder gun) moves forward near St-Léger. The Firefly was the only British tank with sufficient firepower to be able to knock out the larger German panzers from anything other than point-blank range. *(IWM B5416)*

The view from
the woods
south of Ducy-
Ste-Marguerite,
looking towards
Point 103.
This was the
route used by
the Sherwood
Rangers to
outflank
resistance at le
Bas d'Audrieu
on 8 June. The
Rangers crossed
the railway at
the bridge ahead
and then moved
forward to Point
103 by early
evening. *(Author)*

At 2230 hours on 7 June, Maj-Gen Graham's headquarters issued the codeword 'Yar'. This was the signal for all units of 8th Armoured Brigade to disengage and assemble in the area between Brécy and Martragny, north of the N13 near St-Léger. From there, the following morning, they were to attack in accordance with XXX Corps' plan to drive a mobile spearhead to the dominating high ground north-east of Villers-Bocage. Since the brigade's motor infantry battalion was still in England, 50th Division committed 1st Dorsets as infantry support. Additional reinforcement was provided in the form of 288th Anti-Tank Battery (102nd Anti-Tank Regiment), a platoon of 505th Field Company, RE, and most of 2nd Cheshires' A Company. These sub-units would assist in holding the final objective until the brigade group was relieved by 7th Armoured Division. Although understrength, 61st Recce Regiment was also attached to help lead the attack and to send out patrols after a 'firm base' was established near Villers-Bocage. The advance was to take place along two parallel roads, selected before D-Day by Brigadier H.B. Cracroft, 8th Armoured Brigade's commander. The right hand axis, code-named 'Congo', ran from Loucelles via Audrieu and Juvigny to Villers-Bocage. The other route lay through Putot-en-Bessin, Fontenay-le-Pesnel and Monts, and was called 'Isel'. Cracroft also identified two intermediate objectives for his forces. The first of these was the high ground from Point 103 to Point 102,

3–4 km north-east of Tilly-sur-Seulles; this was phase line 'Thames'. The second line ran from Juvigny to Point 111 (2.5 km south-east of Tilly), and was code-named 'Ouse'. The high ground at Villers-Bocage itself was known as objective 'Shannon'.

One of Cracroft's main reasons for choosing minor routes east of the River Seulles for his advance was his desire to side-step enemy reinforcements moving north towards Bayeux. However, by 8 June the arrival of substantial German reserves rendered his choice an unsatisfactory one. Barely had 8th Armoured Brigade's attack begun, than it ran into trouble. Heading east along the Bayeux–Caen highway, 24th Lancers' Reconnaissance Troop met heavy resistance near Putot-en-Bessin, and quickly lost a light tank. The Lancers' B and C Squadrons moved forward in support but, although they killed or captured about 30 SS panzer-grenadiers, they were unable to make significant progress. Meanwhile, after advancing a short distance down Route Congo, 61st Reconnaissance Regiment and 24th Lancers' A Squadron ran up against stiff opposition from remnants of Battle Group *Meyer* and 12th SS Reconnaissance Battalion at Loucelles and le Bas d'Audrieu. 61st Reconnaissance Regiment's commander, Lt-Col Sir William Mount, was shot in the thigh, and the 24th Lancers also suffered several officer and NCO casualties. Despite artillery support from 86th and 147th Field Regiments, and reinforcement by 4th/7th Royal Dragoon Guards, by mid-afternoon 8th Armoured Brigade was still not across the railway at any point.

The Château Maisons, headquarters of I/GR 726. The building was captured by 2nd Devons, attacking across the water meadows from the right (north) on the evening of 8 June. Around 40 prisoners were taken. *(Author)*

Faced with more resistance than he had anticipated, Cracroft decided to abandon the more easterly axis, request additional support and concentrate on opening Route Congo. Deteriorating weather ruled out direct air support, but from 1900 hours the cruisers *Ajax*, *Argonaut* and *Orion* carried out several shoots against the Audrieu area, inflicting heavy losses on the SS defenders. At 1600 hours 1st Dorsets also moved into action, helping 4th/7th RDG capture Loucelles. As darkness fell, the Dorsets' C and D Companies then worked closely with the Dragoon Guards' A Squadron to by-pass German resistance at le Bas d'Audrieu. By midnight, the British had established themselves in Audrieu, as well as at the railway crossing further north. Meanwhile, in a more ambitious outflanking movement, the Sherwood Rangers' tanks advanced to the railway line 1.5 km east of the River Seulles. Finding an unguarded road bridge (there was a gap in the German reconnaissance screen in this area), by early evening they moved south to Point 103, seizing this key feature before nightfall. To consolidate his gains, Brigadier Cracroft ordered 288th Anti-Tank Battery and 2nd Cheshires' machine guns to occupy Point 103 overnight. Although some Germans remained in Audrieu, faced with the outflanking of their defences most withdrew to Cristot, 2 km to the south-east. Consequently, the SS reconnaissance battalion's command post at the Château d'Audrieu was abandoned. Amidst the wreckage of burned out vehicles and fallen trees, the Germans left the bodies of 24 Canadian and two British prisoners, shot in cold blood earlier in the day on the orders of *SS-Sturmbannführer* (Major) Gerhard Bremer, commanding 12th SS Reconnaissance Battalion.

8 June saw mixed fortunes for the rest of 50th Division. There was little to report from the areas occupied by 69th Brigade, 151st Brigade and most of 56th Brigade. The largest clash was 3 km north-west of Bayeux where, after failing to occupy Sully on D+1, 2nd SWB tried again on D+2. At 1215 hours the Borderers' A and B Companies approached Sully from the east, joined by 5th Royal Tank Regiment's A Squadron, which had landed with other elements of 7th Armoured Division on 7 June.

Fire support came from 5th Royal Horse Artillery (also of 7th Armoured Division), plus eight 4.2-inch mortars from 2nd Cheshires' D Company. Initially all went well, with the crossroads 500 metres east of the River Drôme secured against light opposition. However, although resistance in Sully was overcome by Major J.T. Boon's B Company, when A Company crossed the bridge it came under heavy fire from the fortified château west of the river. The Borderers' CO, Lt-Col R.W. Craddock, was wounded, and all attempts to press home the attack failed. When German self-propelled guns appeared from the north, destroying a Sherman Firefly and temporarily cutting off A Company, it was decided to end the battle. Covered by smoke, A Company withdrew across the Drôme. 2nd SWB's C Company then moved forward to occupy the east bank of the river, leaving elements of 726th Grenadier Regiment in control of the west.

For the Germans, the defensive success at Sully represented their last achievement north of Bayeux. By 8 June US V Corps had broken out of its initial lodgement at Omaha Beach, and was making steady progress inland. Simultaneously, the fall of Port-en-Bessin meant the loss of the defenders' last bastion between the invading armies. With 2nd Devons moving unopposed along the coast from the east, the Germans found themselves being squeezed into a pocket of rapidly decreasing dimensions. Despite the arrival by bicycle of several hundred men from 30th Mobile Brigade (*Schnelle Brigade 30*), these lightly armed personnel could do nothing to stop the Allied advance. Consequently, on the afternoon of D+2 GenLt Kraiss ordered Colonel Korfes to continue fighting until nightfall, and then retreat to the south-west. After losing the Château Maisons (I/ GR 726's command post) to an attack by 2nd Devons at 1910 hours, the Germans began their withdrawal, abandoning GR 726's headquarters at Sully and moving south in a long column of vehicles and men on foot. At about 0300 hours on 9 June these troops crossed the N13 at St-Anne, 2 km west of Vaucelles, fighting a frantic battle against US troops in order to escape. Meanwhile, 6 km further north, the first direct British–American encounter

A 2nd Cheshires' Vickers machine-gun team near Audrieu. *(IWM B5439)*

took place at dusk on 8 June, when two officers from 47 RM Commando met American troops near the village of Huppain. The following morning, when 2nd SWB's patrols crossed the river again at Sully, they found the area almost deserted. A few hours later firm contact was established between 56th Brigade and US 1st Infantry Division, and the junction between First US Army and British Second Army was complete. The link-up was three days later than intended, but a notable achievement nonetheless.

On 9 June, 8th Armoured Brigade continued its attempts to push south. During the morning 1st Dorsets and 4th/7th RDG consolidated their hold on Audrieu. The brigade's headquarters moved forward to Point 103, as did 147th Field Regiment and 24th Lancers. Riding on the back of the Lancers' tanks were the infantrymen of 8th DLI, detached from 151st Brigade to lead the attack towards Point 111 (objective Ouse) later in the day. At 1745 hours, after a preliminary artillery bombardment, the Durhams advanced downhill from Point 103, supported by a squadron of Sherman tanks (*see Tour D, pp. 169–85*). By mid-evening, the battalion had ejected elements of the Panzer Lehr Division from the village of St-Pierre, barely 1 km east of Tilly-sur-Seulles. Meanwhile, west of the River Seulles, 56th Brigade was instructed to join 7th Armoured Division, whose 22nd Armoured Brigade was under orders to attack the following morning towards the villages of Hottot and Juvigny, 2 km south of Tilly. 231st Brigade also shifted position,

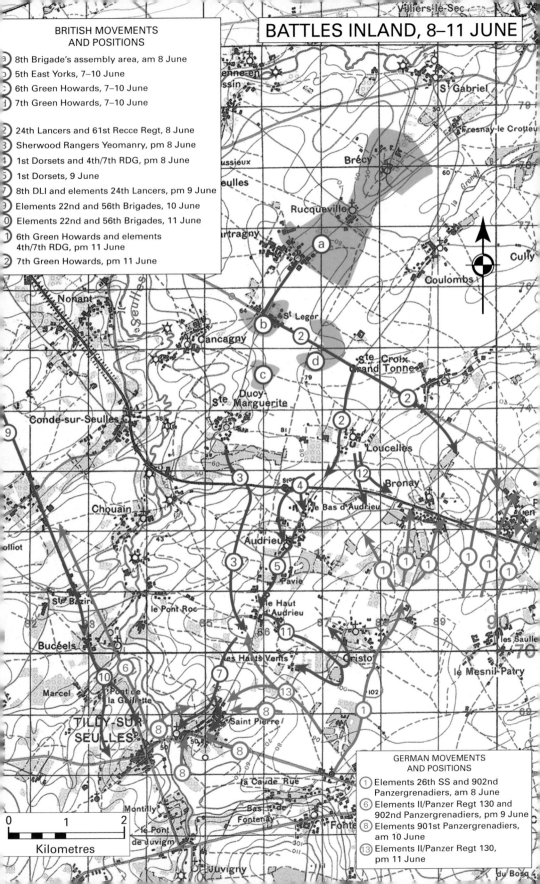

BATTLES INLAND, 8–11 JUNE

BRITISH MOVEMENTS AND POSITIONS

(a) 8th Brigade's assembly area, am 8 June
(b) 5th East Yorks, 7–10 June
(c) 6th Green Howards, 7–10 June
(d) 7th Green Howards, 7–10 June

(2) 24th Lancers and 61st Recce Regt, 8 June
(3) Sherwood Rangers Yeomanry, pm 8 June
(4) 1st Dorsets and 4th/7th RDG, pm 8 June
(5) 1st Dorsets, 9 June
(7) 8th DLI and elements 24th Lancers, pm 9 June
(9) Elements 22nd and 56th Brigades, 10 June
(10) Elements 22nd and 56th Brigades, 11 June
(11) 6th Green Howards and elements 4th/7th RDG, pm 11 June
(12) 7th Green Howards, pm 11 June

GERMAN MOVEMENTS AND POSITIONS

(1) Elements 26th SS and 902nd Panzergrenadiers, am 8 June
(6) Elements II/Panzer Regt 130 and 902nd Panzergrenadiers, pm 9 June
(8) Elements 901st Panzergrenadiers, am 10 June
(13) Elements II/Panzer Regt 130, pm 11 June

Villiers-le-Sec
S¹ Gabriel
Fresnay-le-Crotteu
Brécy
Rucqueville
Cully
Coulombs
Nonant
S¹ Léger
Cancagny
S¹° Croix Grand Tonne
Duoy-S¹° Marguerite
Loucelles
Bronay
Condé-sur-Seulles
le Bas d'Audrieu
Chouain
Audrieu
Pavie
S¹° Bazir
le Pont Roc
le Haut d'Audrieu
Bucéels
les Saulle
Marcel
Pont de la Guillette
les Hauts Vents
Cristo
le Mesnil-Patry
TILLY-SUR-SEULLES
Saint Pierre
la Caude Rue
Montilly
Bas de Fontenay
le Pont de Juvigm
Fonte
Juvigny
du Bosq

0   1   2
Kilometres

The Panzer
Lehr Division's
counter-attack
on 9 June was
regarded as
significant by
the Germans,
but caused the
British little
concern. This is
one of several
Panzer IVs
knocked out that
day. The 'skirts'
around the
hull and turret
were designed
to detonate
hollow-charge
anti-tank rounds
before they hit
the vehicle itself.
(IWM B5375)

relieving 56th Brigade between the Drôme and the Aure rivers while preparing to protect 7th Armoured Division's right flank when it launched its offensive the next day.

Despite the successes of 9 June, the day provided further signs that XXX Corps was entering a new phase in the Battle of Normandy, during which it would have to fight hard for almost every gain. Having occupied Audrieu during the morning, 1st Dorsets was unable to prevent German infiltration back into the village through the close country to the east. On Cracroft's orders, the battalion abandoned its efforts to clear Route Congo and redeployed in an all-round defensive position near Point 103. Simultaneously, after suffering heavy losses, 8th DLI was instructed to consolidate at St-Pierre, rather than attempting to push further south. Bad weather also kept most Allied aircraft grounded on 9 June, and the Panzer Lehr Division took advantage of this to make its first armoured counter-attack. It involved about 50 Panzer IVs from 2nd Battalion, 130th Panzer Lehr Regiment, supported by some panzergrenadiers. Beginning around midday, these elements tentatively pushed northwards along the road from Tilly to Bayeux, until they were stopped by 6th DLI's 6-pounders and some 102nd Anti-Tank Regiment M10s near Condé-sur-Seulles. Although the Germans called off the attack when the loss of St-Pierre threatened their right flank and pre-empted another planned thrust east of the Seulles (by 901st Panzergrenadier Regiment), it nevertheless provided additional evidence of the increasing strength of the forces facing XXX Corps to the south.

By D+4 it was clear that 8th Armoured Brigade's drive had run out of steam. Following a heavy counter-attack on St-Pierre early on 10 June, which threw Cracroft's forces onto the defensive for the entire day, the brigade was ordered to suspend its attack and concentrate on holding the ground it had already gained. Henceforward, the main offensive impetus would be west of the Seulles, where 7th Armoured Division began its own attempt to reach Villers-Bocage the same day. Initially, this made reasonable progress, penetrating to within a few kilometres of Tilly-sur-Seulles. However, during 11 June both 22nd Armoured Brigade and 56th Brigade met fierce resistance in the *bocage* from substantial elements of the Panzer Lehr Division, and their advance came to a

Youthful German prisoners wait to board the LST that will take them to England on 7 June. *(IWM B5139)*

Royal Engineers from 9th Beach Group make friends with the citizens of Ver-sur-Mer. *(IWM B5254)*

complete halt. Meanwhile, a simultaneous attempt by 50th Division on D+5 to enlarge the salient east of the Seulles also came to grief, when the three battalions of 69th Brigade came up against equally determined opposition in the close country east of Audrieu. Particularly severe losses were suffered by 6th Green Howards, which sustained over 200 casualties in an abortive attempt to reach Point 102 near Cristot. Losses among 4th/7th RDG, which supported the attack, and to 5th East Yorks, as it moved up to relieve 1st Dorsets, were also heavy. After another German armoured counter-attack on the evening of 11 June, this time at Point 103, on 12 June St-Pierre was abandoned, and 8th Armoured Brigade withdrew to rest and refit. Its positions south of Audrieu were handed over to elements of 49th Division, newly arrived in the battle area.

Although 50th Division's contribution to the opening stages of the Battle of Normandy ended in disappointment, this should in no way detract from its immense achievement. At remarkably little cost, it had carved its way through the German coastal defences and captured all its initial objectives. Thanks to its efforts, the beautiful town of Bayeux was seized intact, and so avoided the fate that befell so many of Lower Normandy's other settlements. The division's advance had also provided sufficient room for the supply dumps, airfields and other facilities that were the prerequisite for further progress inland, and through the capture of Arromanches had secured the site of one of the two artificial harbours which were seen as so significant to the Allies' logistical efforts. By aggressive action inland, the division and its attached units had also done much to hamper German plans for a concerted counter-attack, at a time when such an event might conceivably have inflicted great harm on the invasion forces. Although XXX Corps would continue to serve valiantly until the end of the north-west European campaign in May 1945, its achievements in the second week of June 1944 in creating a solid centre to the Allied beachhead were rightly seen as among its most significant in the entire Second World War.

PART THREE

BATTLEFIELD TOURS

GENERAL TOURING INFORMATION

Normandy is a thriving holiday area, with some beautiful countryside, excellent beaches and very attractive architecture (particularly in the case of religious buildings). It was also, of course, the scene of heavy fighting in 1944, and this has had a considerable impact on the tourist industry. To make the most of your trip, especially if you intend visiting non-battlefield sites, we strongly recommend you purchase one of the general Normandy guidebooks that are commonly available. These include: *Michelin Green Guide: Normandy*; *Thomas Cook Travellers: Normandy*; *The Rough Guide to Brittany and Normandy*; *Lonely Planet: Normandy*.

TRAVEL REQUIREMENTS

First, make sure you have the proper documentation to enter France as a tourist. Citizens of European Union countries, including Great Britain, should not usually require visas, but will need to carry and show their passports. Others should check with the French Embassy in their own country before travelling. British citizens should also fill in and take Form E111 (available from main post offices), which deals with entitlement to medical treatment, and all should consider taking out comprehensive travel insurance. France is part of the Eurozone, and you should also check exchange rates before travelling.

GETTING THERE

The most direct routes from the UK to Lower Normandy are by ferry from Portsmouth to Ouistreham (near Caen), and from Portsmouth or Poole to Cherbourg.

Depending on which you choose, and whether you travel by day or night, the crossing takes between four and seven hours. Alternatively, you can sail to Le Havre, Boulogne or Calais and drive the rest of the way. (Travel time from Calais to Caen is about four hours; motorway and bridge tolls may be payable depending on the exact route taken.) Another option is to use the Channel Tunnel. Whichever way you decide to travel, early booking is advised, especially during the summer months.

Although you can of course hire motor vehicles in Normandy, the majority of visitors from the UK or other EU countries will probably take their own. If you do so, you will also need to take: a full driving licence; your vehicle registration document; a certificate of motor insurance valid in France (your insurer will advise on this); spare headlight and indicator bulbs; headlight beam adjusters or tape; a high visibility jacket for use in the event of vehicle breakdown; a warning triangle; and a sticker or number plate identifying which country the vehicle is registered in. Visitors from elsewhere should consult a motoring organisation in their home country for details of the documents and other items they will require.

Normandy's road system is well developed, although there are still a few choke points, especially around the larger towns during rush hour and in the holiday season. As a general guide, in clear conditions it is possible to drive from Cherbourg to Caen in less than two hours.

ACCOMMODATION

Accommodation in Normandy is plentiful and diverse, from cheap campsites to five star hotels in glorious châteaux. However, early booking is advised if you wish to travel between June and August. There are many places to stay near Gold Beach, among them the delightful town of Bayeux, which has around 20 hotels catering to a range of budgets. A variety of accommodation can also be found in Arromanches, Port-en-Bessin and the other coastal resorts. There are campsites at Asnelles, Port-en-Bessin and Martragny, 7 km south-east of Bayeux, and *gîtes*

Above: The Green Howards' memorial, Crépon. The plaques record the names of 179 Green Howards who died in Normandy, 28 of them on D-Day. *(Author)*

in many towns and villages. Alternatively, you can base yourself slightly further afield; the historic city of Caen, for example, has over 60 hotels. Useful contacts include:

French Travel Centre, 178 Piccadilly, London W1J 0AL; tel: 0870 830 2000; web: www.raileurope.co.uk

French Tourist Authority, 444 Madison Avenue, New York, NY 10022 (other offices in Chicago, Los Angeles and Miami);
web: www.francetourism.com

Office de Tourisme Intercommunal de Bayeux, Pont Saint-Jean, 14400 Bayeux; tel: +33 (0)2 31 51 28 28;
web: www.bayeux-tourism.com

Calvados Tourisme, 8 Rue Renoir, 14054 Caen; tel: +33 (0)2 31 27 90 30; web: www.calvados-tourisme.com

Manche Tourisme; web: www.manchetourisme.com
Maison du Tourisme de Cherbourg et du Haut-Cotentin,
    2 Quai Alexandre III, 50100 Cherbourg-Octeville;
    tel: +33 (0)2 33 93 52 02; web: www.ot-cherbourg-
    cotentin.fr
Gîtes de France, La Maison des Gîtes de France et du
    Tourisme Vert, 59 Rue Saint-Lazare, 75 439 Paris Cedex
    09; tel: +33 (0)1 49 70 75 75; web: www.gites-de-france.fr

In Normandy itself there are tourist offices in all the large
towns and many of the small ones, especially along the coast.

BATTLEFIELD TOURING

Each volume in this series contains from four to six
battlefield tours. These are intended to last from a few hours
to a full day apiece. Some are best undertaken using motor
transport, others should be done on foot, and many involve
a mixture of the two. Owing to its excellent infrastructure
and relatively gentle topography, Normandy also makes a
good location for a cycling holiday; indeed, some of our
tours are ideally suited to this method.

    In every case the tour author has visited the area
concerned before the original edition of this book was
published, in 2004. Since then, land use, infrastructure
annd rights of way have altered in some areas, although
this is not necessarily reflected in current French mapping.

The Château d'Audrieu is now one of several luxury hotels near Bayeux. However, on 8 June 1944 it was the scene of one of the worst atrocities in the Battle of Normandy, when 24 Canadian and 2 British prisoners were murdered here by members of 12th SS Panzer Division's reconnaissance battalion. *(Author)*

With care, however, it should not be too difficult to identify those small changes that have occurred and to amend one's route accordingly. If you encounter difficulties in following any tour, we would very much like to hear about it, so we can incorporate changes in future editions. Your comments should be sent to the publisher at the address provided at the front of this book.

To derive maximum value and enjoyment from the tours, we suggest you equip yourself with the following items:

- Appropriate maps. European road atlases can be purchased from a wide range of locations outside France. However, for navigation within Normandy, the French Institut Géographique National (IGN) produces maps at a variety of scales (www.ign. fr). The 1:100,000 series ('Top 100') is particularly useful when driving over larger distances; sheet 06 (Caen – Cherbourg) covers most of the invasion area. For pinpointing locations precisely, the current IGN 1:25,000 Série Bleue is best. Extracts from map editions available in 2004 were used for the tour maps in this series, although in a few cases newer editions have appeared since then. These maps can be purchased in many places across Normandy and from specialist

Many of the lanes near Bayeux have changed little since June 1944, when this photo was taken. It shows a 6-pounder anti-tank gun, towed by a 102nd Anti-Tank Regiment Universal Carrier. *(IWM B5374)*

dealers in the UK (e.g. www.themapcentre.com or www.stanfords.co.uk). Allow at least a fortnight's notice, as maps are not always in stock.

- Lightweight waterproof clothing and robust footwear are essential, especially for touring in the countryside.
- Take a compass, provided you know how to use one!
- A camera and spare memory cards.
- A notebook to record what you have photographed.
- A French dictionary and/or phrasebook. (English is widely spoken in the coastal area, but is much less common inland.)
- Food and drink. Although you are never very far in Normandy from a shop, restaurant or *tabac*, many of the tours do not pass directly by such facilities. It is therefore sensible to take some light refreshment with you.
- Binoculars. Most officers and some other ranks carried binoculars in 1944. Taking a pair adds a surprising amount of verisimilitude to the touring experience.

SOME DOS AND DON'TS

Battlefield touring can be an extremely interesting and even emotional experience, especially if you have read something about the battles beforehand. In addition, it is fair to say that residents of Normandy are used to visitors, among them battlefield tourers, and generally will do their best to help if you encounter problems. However, many of the tours in this series are off the beaten track, and you can expect some puzzled looks from the locals, especially inland. In all cases we have tried to ensure that tours are on public land, or viewable from public rights of way. However, in the unlikely event that you are asked to leave a site, do so immediately and by the most direct route.

In addition: **Never remove 'souvenirs' from the battlefields.** Even today it is not unknown for farmers to turn up relics of the 1944 fighting. Taking these without

Bayeux street sign, 9 June 1944. *(IWM B5276)*

permission may not only be illegal, but can be extremely dangerous. It also ruins the site for genuine battlefield archaeologists. Anyone returning from France should also remember customs regulations on the import of weapons and ammunition of any kind.

Be especially careful when investigating fortifications. Some of the more frequently-visited sites are well preserved, and several of them have excellent museums. However, both along the coast and inland there are numerous positions that have been left to decay, and which carry risks for the unwary. In particular, remember that many of these places were the scenes of heavy fighting or subsequent demolitions, which may have caused severe (and sometimes invisible) structural damage. Coastal erosion has also undermined the foundations of a number of shoreline defences. Under no circumstances should underground bunkers, chambers and tunnels be entered, and care should always be taken when examining above-ground structures. If in any doubt, stay away.

Beware of hunting (shooting) areas (signposted *Chasse Gardée*). Do not enter these, even if they offer a short cut to your destination. Similarly, Normandy contains a number of restricted areas (military facilities and wildlife reserves), which should be avoided. Watch out, too, for temporary footpath closures, especially along sections of coastal cliffs.

If using a motor vehicle, keep your eyes on the road. There are many places to park, even on minor routes, and it is always better to turn round and retrace your path than to cause an accident. In rural areas avoid blocking entrances and driving along farm tracks; again, it is better to walk a few hundred metres than to cause damage and offence.

THINGS TO DO IN THE GOLD BEACH AREA

In addition to the superb sandy beaches and resorts, there are many places in the Gold Beach area where families, groups or individuals can spend an enjoyable day out. Bayeux, with its cathedral, famous tapestry, restaurants and shops offers an attractive day's break from battlefield touring. For those who wish to maintain a focus on

Opposite: Arromanches, as seen from the top of WN-43's 105-mm gun casemate. The D-Day Museum is the modern, light-coloured building by the seafront. WN-44 was located on the cliffs west of Arromanches, near the buildings furthest from the camera. Note the offshore reefs and remains of the Mulberry harbour. *(Author)*

military matters, it is also the site of the excellent *Musée Mémorial de la Bataille de Normandie*, covering the entire Battle of Normandy. Very close by, on the opposite side of the ring road, is the largest of Normandy's Commonwealth War Graves Commission cemeteries. It contains 4,748 graves, 3,935 of them British. Most of 50th Division's D-Day dead are laid to rest here. Other CWGC cemeteries are listed in the individual battlefield tours (*see p. 130–31 and p. 184–85*). One that is not, but where soldiers killed during the fighting described in this book are buried, is at Brouay, 11 km south-east of Bayeux, near the N13. The major German war cemetery is at la Cambe, 18 km west of Bayeux (also near the N13), where 21,222 German soldiers, sailors and airmen are buried.

Above: The Château Creully is open to visitors throughout the summer. It was also the site of the BBC's first studio in liberated Normandy, which can be seen in one of the building's towers. (Author)

BATTLE OF NORMANDY MUSEUM

Musée Mémorial de la Bataille de Normandie,
Boulevard Fabian Ware, 14400 Bayeux; tel: +33 (0)2 31 51 46 90;
email: <bataillenormandie@mairie-bayeux.fr>. Open 0930–1830 daily 1 May–30
Sept, otherwise 1000–1230 & 1400–1800 daily, closed for two weeks in Jan.
Entrance fee.

Details of other museums and invasion-related sites are listed in the individual battlefield tours.

This part of Calvados also provides the location for numerous châteaux, abbeys and churches, some of them of great architectural merit. Among the most impressive are the Château de Balleroy (+33 (0)2 31 21 60 61) and the Château de Creully (+33 (0)2 31 80 18 65), both of which open daily throughout the summer. The former is 13 km south-west of Bayeux, and offers beautiful gardens and a hot air balloon museum as well as the château itself. A few kilometres west of Balleroy is the imposing Benedictine abbey of Cerisy-la-Forêt; slightly further east (and 7 km south of Bayeux) you will find the abbey of Mondaye, which is also open to the public. Closer to Gold Beach, the exquisite Église Saint-Aubin at Vaux-sur-Aure (2 km north of Bayeux) is one of many small churches in the area which are worth a visit. For those wishing to see religious architecture on an altogether grander scale, Rouen cathedral and Mont-St-Michel can be visited in a day apiece. The centre of Caen, with numerous sites of historic interest, is about 40 minutes from Bayeux.

Children ought to enjoy many of the places listed above. However, it is also worth mentioning *Parc Festyland*, a theme park on the western side of Caen (web: <www.festyland.com>; tel: +33 (0)2 31 75 04 04), and the indoor go-kart track on the opposite side of Caen (web: <www.karting-caen.fr>; tel: +33 (0)2 31 83 09 53). As with other entertainments and recreational pursuits, further details can be found on the regional tourist websites identified on p. 106–7.

THE GOLD BEACH TOURS

This book contains four battlefield tours, offering a cross-section of 50th Division's experiences on and immediately after D-Day. The only large formation not represented is 56th Infantry Brigade, partly because it fought no major battle before being attached to 7th Armoured Division on 10 June, and partly because the key feature at the site of 2nd South Wales Borderers' action at Sully (on 8 June) – the château used as 726th Grenadier Regiment's headquarters – no longer exists. However, if you are interested in tracing actions other than those described in the tours below, there is no reason why you should not do so. Although land use in some areas has altered since 1944, and most villages and towns have grown, it is remarkable how little has changed in many places. With close attention to the contents of this book, combined with careful map reading, you should be able to discover the exact sites of many of the clashes described in the earlier part of this book. As always, however, please make respect for property and the safety of yourself and others the critical factors influencing your choice of where to visit.

The maps for Tours A and B provide complete coverage of the assault sector of Gold Beach. However, you will probably find it helpful to purchase the relevant Institut Géographique National Série Bleue map sheet (1512 OT 'Bayeux & Arromanches-les-Bains'), which includes the area as far west as Port-en-Bessin and as far south as Tilly-sur-Seulles.

To find out more about the landings on either flank of Gold Beach, please consult the volumes *Omaha Beach* and *Juno Beach* in this series. To discover what happened south of Bayeux after 50th Division's assault, see *Villers-Bocage* in the series.

Memorial to 2nd Battalion, The Hertfordshire Regiment, Espace Robert Kiln, Ver-sur-Mer. As part of 9th Beach Group, 2nd Herts' main task was to ensure the smooth transit of troops and equipment from King sector inland. However, the battalion also helped to mop up la Rivière, losing three men killed in action and another drowned while landing. *(Author)*

KING SECTOR, VER-SUR-MER AND CRÉPON

OBJECTIVE: This tour covers the landings on King sector, in particular the attack and exploitation by 6th Battalion, The Green Howards. It also records two conspicuous acts of gallantry by Company Sergeant-Major (CSM) Stanley Hollis, the only man to be awarded the Victoria Cross (Britain's highest military decoration) for actions carried out on D-Day.

DURATION/SUITABILITY: This tour takes about a day, assuming you start mid-morning – when the museum opens – and break for lunch. The total distance is 13 km, roughly half of it on foot. After very heavy or prolonged rain it is suggested you take Wellington boots to help cross what may be saturated terrain between stands A2 and A3. The tour is suitable for cyclists, although given the proportion of the tour which is off-road, a mountain bike would be more appropriate than a touring bike. For those with mobility difficulties, most points can be seen from the car, but access to Stand A2 is likely to be difficult.

STARTING THE TOUR: The best place to start is the *Musée America Gold Beach* in Ver-sur-Mer (follow the signposts in Ver or use the map opposite). This outstanding museum records the planning and execution of the assault on Gold Beach. It also commemorates the arrival in July 1927 of the pioneering US aviator

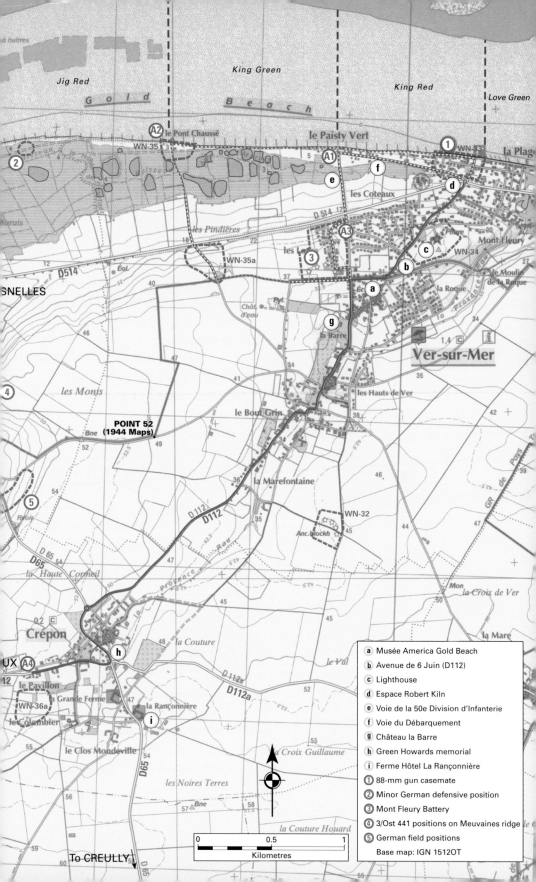

Jig Red   *King Green*   *King Red*   *Love Green*
G   o   l   d   B   e   a   c   h

Ⓐ2 le Pont Chaussé   le Paisty Vert   ① WN-33   la Plag
WN-35 ③   ⑤   Ⓐ1   la Plag
②   ⑤   Ⓐ1   ⓕ   ⓓ
les Coteaux
ⓔ
D 514   17   Mont Fleury   20
les Pindières   18   Ⓐ3   WN-35a   ⓒ   WN-34   27
NELLES   12   D514   Ⓐ3   37   ⓑ   la Roque   le Moulin de la Roque
40   Chât.   Pyl.   ⓐ   34
d'eau   ⓖ   la Barre   1,4 Ⓒ ℹ
46   47   34   Ver-sur-Mer   35
④   les Monis   41   les Hauts de Ver   38   42
POINT 52
(1944 Maps)   le Bout Grin   34
52   49
la Marefontaine   46
⑤   35   WN-32   44   47
Rfois   D 112   45   39
D 65   54   Anc.blockh   45
la Haute Cormeil   47   la Croix de Ver
50
45   45   la Mare
Crépon   0,2 Ⓒ   48   la Couture   le Val
UX Ⓐ4   ⓗ   le Val
12   le Pavillon   D 112a   52
WN-36a   Grande Ferme   47   la Rançonnière
le Colombier   ⓘ   D 112a
le Clos Mondeville   54   la Croix Guillaume   55
D 65   les Noires Terres
57   Bne   58

ⓐ Musée America Gold Beach
ⓑ Avenue de 6 Juin (D112)
ⓒ Lighthouse
ⓓ Espace Robert Kiln
ⓔ Voie de la 50e Division d'Infanterie
ⓕ Voie du Débarquement
ⓖ Château la Barre
ⓗ Green Howards memorial
ⓘ Ferme Hôtel La Rançonnière
① 88-mm gun casemate
② Minor German defensive position
③ Mont Fleury Battery
④ 3/Ost 441 positions on Meuvaines ridge
⑤ German field positions
   Base map: IGN 1512OT

0   0.5   1
Kilometres

To CREULLY

GOLD BEACH MUSEUM

Musée America Gold Beach, 2 Place Amiral Byrd, 14114 Ver-sur-Mer;
tel/fax: +33 (0)2 31 21 09 12; www.goldbeachmusee.org.uk. Open 1030–1730
daily July & Aug; closed Tues April, May, June, Sept & Oct, otherwise hours 1030–
1700; open by appointment Nov–March. Entrance fee.

Richard Byrd, who ditched his aircraft *America* off Mont Fleury after an epic transatlantic flight. The museum incorporates a tourist information centre.

After visiting the museum, drive north-east along the Avenue de 6 Juin (D112), passing the Mont Fleury lighthouse 100 metres to your right, and park at the Espace Robert Kiln. There are several interesting things to see here, including memorials, information boards and a Sexton self-propelled gun. Facilities include a pharmacy and a bar serving light meals. The house next to the pharmacy – one of only a small number in la Rivière to survive D-Day – was occupied briefly by Admiral Ramsay (Allied Naval C-in-C), and bears a commemorative plaque on its gatepost.

Cross the D514 and walk down the Avenue du Colonel Harper to the seafront. Here you will find two relics of WN-33. The first is an octagonal emplacement, built into the sea wall, which held a 50-mm anti-tank gun on D-Day. This position has been converted into a lifeguards' tower. Turning left along the Boulevard de la Plage, you can see the 88-mm anti-tank gun casemate that was responsible for destroying two British AVREs (*see pp. 63–4*). Walk to this position and observe its field of fire to the west.

STAND A1: LE PAISTY VERT

DIRECTIONS: From the 88-mm gun emplacement, continue 750 metres west to the concrete ramp at le Paisty Vert. The most direct route is along the top of the beach, past the area (King Red) where Z Breaching Squadron (elements of 81st Assault Squadron, RE, and six Sherman Crabs from C Squadron, The Westminster Dragoons), 5th East Yorks and C Squadron, 4th/7th Royal Dragoon Guards, landed on D-Day.

A few metres inland from the ramp, at a sandy crossroads, you will see a small stone building. This was once a shelter for passengers using the light railway that ran along the coast to Asnelles. On D-Day it was the only building in the immediate area, and was unoccupied. Since it stood at the entrance to one of only two existing routes across the marsh, the British planners identified it (not unreasonably) as a German pillbox, and allocated two LCG(L)s to its destruction. Two destroyers also shelled this position an hour before the assault troops landed. As you can see, however, the shelter is still very much intact!

Look out to sea across the beach to the west; for the next kilometre this is King Green.

THE ACTION: The first personnel to disembark on King Green, just before 0725 hours, were nine frogmen from LCOCU 3, under the command of Lieutenant H.T. Hargreaves, RNVR. Landing in less than a metre of water, they began to demolish beach obstacles in the shallows, clearing six steel hedgehogs in the first few minutes. They were followed closely by three LCTs carrying X Breaching Squadron, comprising a variety of AVREs, Crabs and an armoured bulldozer, plus 77 men from 280th Field Company, and by the 19 DD Shermans of B Squadron, 4th/7th RDG. Because of the rough seas, the DD tanks were brought inshore to execute a deep wade (like X Breaching Squadron, they landed in almost two metres of water), instead of being launched over 6,000 metres out, as the plan suggested. While these vehicles were disembarking, the first flight of 10 LCAs arrived, carrying the two leading companies of 6th Green Howards, as well as 26 engineers from 233rd Field Company and a forward observation team from 342nd Battery, 86th Field Regiment.

Naval reports state that there was no German reaction on King Beach at the beginning of the assault, almost certainly because of the neutralising effects of the fire support. Consequently, although an AVRE and several DD tanks were flooded, and many of 280th Field Company's

Le Paisty Vert. The photograph provides an approximation of the view seen by 6th Green Howards' D Company as it advanced up the beach soon after 0730 hours on 6 June. *(Author)*

Below: The railway halt, le Paisty Vert. In 1944 the area between the halt and the seashore (on the far side of the white building) was sown with anti-personnel and anti-tank mines, part of the minefield that extended the length of Gold Beach. *(Author)*

boats capsized as they were towed ashore by the AVREs, almost all the British armour reached the water's edge intact. So did most of 6th Green Howards' D and A Companies (unfortunately, several men drowned), which began to cross the beach towards the sandy bank at the high water mark. D Company landed close to where you are standing; A Company was about 250 metres further west.

Before the troops reached the dunes, however, the Germans started to recover, dropping mortar bombs and bullets among the figures stumbling across the sand. Nevertheless, although a number of men were killed or wounded (including 6th Green Howards' beachmaster, Major Jackson, and several NCOs), most arrived unharmed at the top of the beach. Among them were Major Lofthouse,

Then: British troops head inland from King Green towards 'Lavatory Pan Villa'. Note the Sherman Crab and AVRE on the left. Mont Fleury battery was to the right of the house and 200 metres further inland. The significance of the house as a landmark is obvious. *(IWM MH2323)*

Now (below): A view from the bottom of the same road in 2004. Lavatory Pan Villa is to the right of the road, behind one of the two large white houses. *(Author)*

CSM Hollis and almost all of D Company. Here, under the cover of dust and smoke from the still burning grass, they paused to consider their next move.

Major R.L. Jackson, 6th Green Howards' Unit Landing Officer (or beachmaster) landed with D Company at about 0730 hours.

'At every step we expected to be fired at, but were not. The lack of opposition became eerie. Then, after about 200 yards, we must have reached a German fixed line for suddenly they threw everything at us. The mortars took us first and I was hit badly in the leg. My radio operator and [military] policeman were both killed outright by the same explosion . . .

The first wave of infantry passed me by, and the next, and after a time the field of fire receded...

It was the worst moment of the war for me. I could not move and no one was there to drag me beyond the high tide mark. The water came swirling in until it covered my dead companions. Then it lapped my legs and reached my chest. It was a clear sunny day, but the sea was icy cold – or so it seemed. I knew I was badly wounded, but not mortally so, and it seemed absurd to die like that in inches of water.

Quite suddenly our sergeant of regimental police, from my home town, came along the beach, saw me in time and carried me to a sand dune where I lay for the rest of the day.'

Source: Normandy, D-Day: With the Green Howards of the 50th Division, p. 27.

Since the beach exit itself was undefended, and despite enemy fire, 233rd Field Company's 'thug parties' were able quickly to cut the wire and clear gaps through the lateral minefield in front of the coastal road. Although two Sherman Crabs were damaged here (at least one by the 88-mm gun at WN-33), meaning that vehicles could not cross the minefield at this point, D Company passed through these gaps and into the marsh area. Here it re-organised for its next task, the attack on the Mont Fleury Battery.

At around 0750 hours 6th Green Howards' reserve companies (C and B), together with more engineers and two machine-gun sections (part of 2nd Cheshires' B Company) landed from the second flight of LCAs approximately 400 metres to the west and advanced to join the assault. Crossing the sands, they suffered losses to mortar fire, including the commander of C Company, Captain Jack Linn. Wounded on the beach, he courageously directed his men from a sitting position until injured again, this time fatally.

STAND A2: WIDERSTANDSNEST 35

DIRECTIONS: Continue west along the shoreline for about 1 km to WN-35 (le Pont Chaussé on modern maps). Here you will find several pillboxes and bunkers, plus the remains of other positions on the beach (the result of coastal erosion). Most of these appear intact, although they are filled with rubbish and sand and should not be entered. In 1944 there was a 1–3 metre high sea wall along this section of beach (it ended about 100 metres east of the position); this is no longer present. As a result the coastal road that ran through WN-35 has been washed away.

A Company, 6th Green Howards, was tasked with capturing this resistance nest, which was suspected from aerial photographs to contain six pillboxes and at least one artillery piece, protected on all sides except the north by wire and mines. Since it represented the largest shoreline position between WN-33 and WN-36 (near le Hamel), WN-35 was hit heavily before H-hour, first by four destroyers, next by two LCT(R)s and finally – during the assault itself – by several close support vessels. Shortly before the landings began it was also the target for three

This aerial photograph shows the German platoon position at WN-35 soon after its capture. Note the three tanks in the centre of the strongpoint, the vehicles and personnel on the beach and coast road, and the track inland towards WN-35a. (*Keele University Air Photo Archive*)

A German pillbox at WN-35. The embrasure on the left faces onto the beach. The Meuvaines ridge is in the background. (*Author*)

squadrons of heavy bombers, which were supposed to drop 42 tons of bombs (instantaneously fused to avoid cratering the beach) on the position. It is unclear whether or not this raid hit its target.

THE ACTION: After crossing the beach 500 metres east of WN-35, Captain Frederick Honeyman's A Company moved towards its objective. While doing so it came under mortar and machine-gun fire from the garrison, supplemented by stick grenades once the attackers came within range. Faced with intense resistance, and with its commander wounded by splinters, A Company was forced to take cover under the sea wall.

Fortunately, 69th Brigade's operation order had allocated armoured support to the attack. This took the form of three 81st Assault Squadron AVREs, one from each of the LCTs that had landed X Breaching Team a few minutes earlier. Under the command of Captain D.A. King, RE, these negotiated the beach obstacles and approached WN-35, firing their Besa machine guns and petard mortars at the pillboxes. They were supported by at least one DD Sherman from B Squadron, 4th/7th RDG.

With the majority of the German heavy weapons neutralised (among them a 50-mm anti-tank gun), A Company and the AVREs stormed the position. A Company was led by Captain Honeyman, despite his wounds, together with Lance-Sergeant Prenty and Lance-Corporal Joyce, who threw grenades over the parapet and then leapt into the strongpoint, their guns blazing. After a short fight the surviving defenders surrendered. (Honeyman was awarded the MC; Prenty and Joyce both received the MM. Sadly, Honeyman was killed on 11 June, during the attack on Cristot.)

While A Company mopped up WN-35, Major J.M. Young's B Company (from the second flight) moved up the track to the quarry position on the ridge (WN-35a), capturing it after a brief fight. The company then moved to the right, clearing some of 3/Ost 441's dugouts towards Meuvaines, before joining the battalion in its re-organising area at Point 52 (Point 49 on modern maps), half-way between Meuvaines and Ver. From here, at approximately 1130 hours, 6th Green Howards moved forward towards its second phase objectives.

STAND A3: LAVATORY PAN VILLA

DIRECTIONS: Leave WN-35 by the track shown in the photograph below. After 700 metres cross the D514, looking out for fast moving traffic, and continue uphill towards the clump of trees. This marks the position of WN-35a. Note the superb fields of fire from this general area towards the beach.

At the trees, turn left (east) along a farm track/footpath. Walk 500 metres, passing a water tower to your right, and enter the Rue des Roquettes via a gate at the end of the track. Look 150 metres right to a stone wall. On 6 June 1944 this was where three 122-mm guns (Russian pieces captured on the Eastern Front) from the Mont Fleury Battery (3/HKAA 1260) were dug in, ready to be moved into their

The access track from WN-35 to WN-35a, approximately 1 km distant. *(Author)*

casemates once these were completed. According to British reports, the intensity of the pre-assault bombardment meant that none of these guns fired on D-Day.

Continue east along the Rue des Roquettes. Looking left you can see two incomplete concrete structures, which were part of the Mont Fleury Battery (*see top photo p. 23*). These are on farmland, but a good view can be gained from the road. Go to the crossroads at the end of the Rue des Roquettes, and turn left along Avenue F.D. Roosevelt. After 50 metres turn left again into Allée H. Berlioz. The only one of the Mont Fleury casemates to have been ready for action by 6 June can be seen here.

Continue north through the housing estate along the Rue Claude Debussy. This runs on top of an old German communications trench before bearing right to join the Avenue F.D. Roosevelt. Walk towards this road junction, looking right until you see a house with red gates and shutters. This is 'Lavatory Pan Villa' (so-called because of the circular shape of its driveway, viewed from the air), which stands next to the site of the first of two D-Day actions that led to CSM Hollis being awarded the Victoria Cross.

THE ACTION: Roughly an hour after landing, D Company moved inland from its shoreline positions, crossing the marsh and anti-tank ditch and approaching the Mont Fleury Battery. Two platoons were deployed forward, with the third in reserve. Major Ronnie Lofthouse, company commander, and his CSM, Stan Hollis, followed the leading troops.

Ignoring the unoccupied Lavatory Pan Villa, the assault platoons continued towards the casemates, probably along the road immediately to the east (now the Avenue F.D. Roosevelt). However, as Lofthouse and Hollis approached a wall 50 metres in front of the house, Lofthouse detected a bunker a short distance to his right. Conscious that any weapon placed there might be able to hit the assault platoons from the rear as they attacked their objective, the two men went to investigate. However, barely had they begun to move towards the position, when they came under heavy fire from it.

Without pausing, Hollis dashed forward, firing his sub-machine gun. Somehow surviving the hail of bullets, he reached the bunker and clambered onto its roof. He then slipped a grenade through its embrasure, waited a few seconds for the explosion, and jumped down into the trench at the rear entrance. Dashing inside, he found two Germans dead and several others concussed, whom he took prisoner.

This aerial photograph was taken on 4 June 1944. Although it does not show the effects of the D-Day bombardment, some of which struck the area between the anti-tank ditch and the Mont Fleury Battery casemates, it shows clearly Lavatory Pan Villa and the German trench system next to it. *(Keele Air Photo Archive)*

Key

a. Railway halt, le Paisty Vert
b. 50th Infantry Division Way
c. Anti-tank ditch
d. Incomplete road (modern D514)
e. Lavatory Pan Villa
f. Possible site of first bunker attacked by CSM Hollis
g. German communication trench
h. Possible site of second bunker from which Germans surrendered to CSM Hollis
i. Mont Fleury Battery

The most easterly of the Mont Fleury casemates, seen from the Allée H. Berlioz. The casemate was hit by a 500-lb bomb, which caused a large crater above the shell room. The gun in this casemate fired only three rounds on D-Day. (Author)

Having cleared the position, Hollis continued south along a communications trench, changing his magazine as he went. As he approached another bunker, more Germans emerged from it. Fortunately for all concerned, they were in no mood to fight (they may have witnessed the incident a few minutes earlier), and Hollis accepted their surrender.

CSM Hollis' bravery made a significant contribution to the capture of the Mont Fleury position, which was mopped up with little resistance by 0930 hours. Later in the day he would demonstrate similar gallantry in the village of Crépon. This action is covered at Stand A4.

Although sporadic mortar and shell fire continued to fall among the troops landing on King Beach, by 1030 hours 6th Green Howards had secured the shoreline positions west of WN-33, as well as most of the Meuvaines Ridge (C Company passing through D to seize Point 52). With the capture of la Rivière by 5th East Yorks, a breakthrough had been achieved on the eastern half of Gold Beach. For the rest of the day a steady stream of personnel and vehicles, including the rest of 69th Brigade, plus 151st Brigade and many support units, was able to land here without significant interference. The passage of vehicles inland was greatly eased after an AVRE commanded by Captain T.W. Davis laid a 10-metre standard box girder bridge over a crater on the road 200 metres inland from Lavatory Pan Villa, and when a Sherman Crab (Lieutenant B. Pear) flailed a path from the house to the quarry at WN-35a, thus enabling traffic using this exit to detour around the congestion in Ver-sur-Mer.

STAND A4: LE PAVILLON FARM

DIRECTIONS: Return to le Paisty Vert down the Voie de la 50e Division d'Infanterie (50th Infantry Division Way), taking care crossing the D514. At Stand A1 turn right (east) along the Voie du Débarquement. In 1944 this was the main coastal road connecting la Rivière and Asnelles. Continue for 1 km to the Espace Robert Kiln.

By car, head inland along the D112 (Avenue de 6 Juin). Follow the short one-way system (right into the Rue du Moulin, then left on the Avenue Paul Poret) towards the centre of Ver. Continue south, immediately passing two restaurants and – on your right – an attractive château. Proceed for 1 km, taking care as the road winds its way through the village. Ver's church tower is to your left, and is worth a visit; there is a car park opposite.

You may also want to make a detour to see the battery positions (of 6/AR 1716) at WN-32, some 500 metres east of la Marefontaine (use the tour map to help you). WN-32 was captured by 7th Green Howards' C Company, assisted by two Churchill Crocodiles from 13th Troop, C Squadron, 141st Regiment RAC, (using their 75-mm guns, not their flame-throwers). These elements landed on King Green at 0820 hours as part of 69th Brigade's reinforcement. Four 100-mm guns and 50 prisoners were taken at WN-32,

The château at Ver-sur-Mer (la Barre). The building was used as 9th Beach Group's headquarters from 7 June onwards. *(Author)*

which had been heavily shelled (by HMS *Belfast*) and bombed earlier that morning.

Exit Ver-sur-Mer on the D112; on D-Day this was 6th Green Howards' main axis of advance ('Rubicon Road'). Continue to a roundabout on the north-west outskirts of Crépon. Take the second exit (straight ahead), and drive slowly through the village, looking out for the Green Howards' memorial on your left, on the corner of the Rue d'Église (*see photo p. 106*). Park near the statue and read the inscriptions. The churchyard 100 metres away contains two RAF war graves.

Continue for about 50 metres along the D112 to a crossroads. Turn right (signposted Bayeux – still the D112) and proceed for 600 metres to the entrance of le Pavillon farm on your left.

This is the scene of the second of the two actions that won CSM Hollis his VC. It is best viewed from within the farm, with the owner's permission. If the owner is absent, it is just possible to see the scene of the action from the property next door.

THE ACTION: Crépon was reached by 6th Green Howards (less C Company, which moved south-west to capture WN-35b) soon after midday. Resistance was encountered on the outskirts. Because of the need to maintain momentum the battalion's commander, Lt-Col Robin Hastings, ordered most of his men to by-pass the village and continue towards their next objective, Villiers-le-Sec. However, conscious of the requirement to secure a path through Crépon, which lay astride 69th Brigade's axis of advance, he instructed Major Lofthouse's D Company to comb through the village.

Advancing from the north-east, D Company soon approached Crépon's western exit at le Pavillon farm. By now CSM Hollis was leading 16 Platoon, its commander (Lieutenant J.A. Kirkpatrick) having been killed near the Mont Fleury Battery and its platoon sergeant (J.J. 'Rufty' Hill) drowned while coming ashore. Hollis took some of his men through the main gate of le Pavillon farm to search its buildings. Having investigated the farmhouse, where he found a frightened boy, Hollis returned to the yard. Noticing a passageway between the house and a high stone wall, he led his men down it. After a few seconds they reached a small outbuilding next to an orchard.

Looking round the corner, Hollis heard a loud bang as a bullet struck the wall next to him. Ducking down, he could see a hedge at the southern end of the orchard, about 150 metres away. Two dogs wagging their tails indicated a human presence, and Hollis thought he could see an artillery piece. He decided to return to the road to collect a grenade launcher (a 'Projector, Infantry, Anti-Tank', or PIAT for short), with which to try to destroy the gun.

Having found a PIAT and received Lofthouse's permission to make the attempt, Hollis returned to the passageway, ordering several men to rush into the orchard and provide covering fire while he crawled through a rhubarb patch with two Bren gunners to engage the Germans. As Hollis and his colleagues moved forward, however, there were no protecting volleys, the other soldiers having been killed or wounded. Despite this, Hollis continued until he reached a position from which he thought he might hit the artillery piece. He braced the PIAT against his shoulder and fired.

To his disappointment, the round fell short. Effectively disarmed (the PIAT was difficult to reload), Hollis watched with horror as the field gun barrel was lowered until it seemed to point straight at him. Fortunately, at such a short distance he was beneath the gun's angle of maximum depression. Consequently, when it fired, the shell went straight over Hollis' head and into the house behind.

Deciding it was time for a tactical withdrawal, Hollis yelled to the Bren gunners to follow him, and crawled back to the passageway. However, when he reached the road he could still hear firing from the far side of the house, and realised his men had been unable to get out. Grabbing another Bren gun, he returned to the orchard, dashed into the middle and stood in full view of the enemy, providing covering fire while his comrades retreated. Thanks to Hollis' bravery all three men made it back to

Above: The entrance to le Pavillon farm. The passageway referred to in the text is at the end of the farmhouse furthest from the camera. *(Author)*

their company. Quite understandably, this time Major Lofthouse decided it was better to leave the German strongpoint for follow-on forces to deal with. D Company therefore left Crépon and pushed on to the south.

This is the concluding paragraph from CSM Hollis' Victoria Cross citation.

'Wherever fighting was heaviest CSM Hollis appeared, and in the course of a magnificent day's work he displayed the utmost gallantry, and on two separate occasions his courage and initiative prevented the enemy from holding up the advance at critical stages. It was largely through his heroism and resource that the Company's objectives were gained and casualties were

Left: The view from the passageway entrance, looking towards the stone outbuilding and orchard a few metres away. *(Author)*

not heavier, and by his own bravery he saved the lives of many of his men.'

Source: W.A.T. Synge, *The Story of the Green Howards*, p. 293.

Despite further mopping up by 5th East Yorks and 7th Green Howards, the German position south-west of Crépon – WN-36a – was not taken until the following morning, by a mixed force of 86th Field Regiment gunners, a flame-throwing 'Crocodile' and several Sherman Crabs. Some 60 prisoners and five artillery pieces were captured, probably from 5/AR 1716.

ENDING THE TOUR: This is the end of the tour. However, you may want to visit the beautiful and moving Ryes-Bazenville war cemetery, approximately 4 km west of Crépon. To get there, continue on the D112 for 3½ km and turn left on the D87. The cemetery is a few hundred metres along the road on the left. It contains 652 Commonwealth war graves (plus one Pole), as well as 326 German graves. Private Derrick Beckwith, who at 19 years old was one of the youngest of the 18 soldiers of 6th Green Howards to be killed on D-Day, is buried here (Block III, D3). Point 62 (Point 64 on wartime maps), which is next to the cemetery, offers outstanding views to the north and west. Another option is to visit the Ferme Hôtel *La Rançonnière* in Crépon, which is marked on the tour map and has a well-reviewed restaurant (+33 (0)2 31 22 21 73; <www.ranconniere.com>).

The view from the stone outbuilding. The rhubarb patch through which Hollis crawled was to the right of the fence on the left hand side of the photograph. The German field gun was somewhere near the gap in the hedge visible in the distance. *(Author)*

JIG SECTOR TO ARROMANCHES

OBJECTIVE: This tour covers the landings on Jig sector, especially the attack and exploitation by 1st Battalion, The Hampshire Regiment.

DURATION/SUITABILITY: The tour lasts about a day, assuming you break for lunch and visit Arromanches. The total distance is 13 km, most of it suitable for cyclists, although there are some short stretches of busy road. For those with mobility difficulties, all stands are accessible by car. The walks along the coast are optional, and the steps at Stand B6 can easily be avoided by driving into Arromanches.

STARTING THE TOUR: The tour starts at Roseau Plage. Your most likely approach is along the D514 coast road. Turn off towards the seafront 1 km east of Asnelles and continue for 600 metres to the car park.

STAND B1: JIG GREEN BEACH

DIRECTIONS: If the tide is out, walk onto the beach using the concrete ramp near the car park. On D-Day this was Jig Green, which was divided into two sectors, east and west. The boundary between them was at WN-36, now partly covered by the car park. Jig Green West stretched 750 metres to le Hamel, and was the intended landing area for 1st Hampshires (and its attached platoon from 295th Field Company), the 19 DD Shermans of B Squadron, The Nottinghamshire

(Sherwood Rangers) Yeomanry, and some of the 'funnies' of 82nd Assault Squadron, RE, and B Squadron, The Westminster Dragoons. In 1944 the area immediately behind Jig Green West was marshland. Since the war this has been reclaimed and covered with the houses and holiday apartments of Roseau Plage. However, the area east of the car park, which for 300 metres was Jig Green East, has hardly changed in the last 60 years. On D-Day this was where 1st Battalion, The Dorsetshire Regiment, and C Squadron, Sherwood Rangers, plus their attached assault engineers, were supposed to disembark.

THE ACTION: According to 231st Brigade's plan, 1st Hampshires and its supporting elements were tasked with capturing the two *Widerstandsnester* (WN-37 and WN-38) at le Hamel, as well as the village of Asnelles. The battalion was then to leave part of its Support Company to hold Asnelles, and push on to take further positions along the coast. These included WN-39 (on the slopes west of Asnelles); *Stützpunkt Arromanche*s; WN-43 (Arromanches East); WN-44 (Arromanches West); the village of Arromanches itself; Tracy-sur-Mer; and Manvieux. Meanwhile, 1st Dorsets would assault WN-36, move inland through les Roquettes and seize the high ground 2 km south-east of Arromanches. The brigade's reserve battalion, 2nd Battalion, The Devonshire Regiment, would land on Jig Green West at H+45 (0810 hours) and advance down the valley of la Gronde Ruisseau (known as la Gronde Riviere in 1944) to Ryes, 3 km from Arromanches. 1st Dorsets would then move to Ryes, freeing 2nd Devons to attack north-westwards along the coast. The aim was to overrun all defences (notably the battery at Longues) as far as Port-en-Bessin, at the western end of Gold Beach. The capture of Port-en-Bessin itself was allocated to 47 RM Commando, which would land at H+2 hours (0925 hours) and infiltrate across country to seize the town. If all went well, by the end of D-Day 231st Brigade would have secured 50th Division's right flank and linked up with US V Corps, advancing east from Omaha Beach. This would

The view from the car park at WN-36, looking east. The concrete wreckage visible on the beach includes parts of the position that was located here. Owing to coastal erosion and post-war clearance, little else remains of this *Widerstandsnest*, which held a 50-mm anti-tank gun, a 37-mm gun, pillboxes and trenches, surrounded on all sides except the north by barbed wire and minefields. (Author)

make a critical contribution to the establishment of a firm lodgement by the Allied armies.

The landings on Jig Green did not go according to plan. Much of the preliminary bombardment that was intended to neutralise WN-37 – which dominated the beach – either did not occur, or missed its target. Owing to the rough seas, the commander of 15th LCT Flotilla was instructed not to launch his DD tanks, but to bring them inshore after the assault engineers and infantry had landed. Consequently, when the first waves of landing craft arrived at 0725 hours, they lacked armoured support and faced a virtually intact strongpoint to their right.

The first vessels to beach on Jig Green West – three of the breaching team LCTs – came under heavy fire even before they grounded. *LCT 886*, carrying engineers to open an exit at WN-37, was hit many times, suffered numerous casualties, and was unable to launch any of its vehicles or disembark its personnel. Although the other LCTs managed to get their AVREs and flails ashore, several vehicles bogged in clay patches on the beach itself or were disabled as they tried to penetrate the coastal minefield. Major Harold Elphinstone, commanding the breaching teams, was killed soon after landing, and the engineers of LCOCU 10 and 73rd Field Company (which landed with the breaching teams) also incurred losses as they tried to clear gaps through the beach obstacles. Of the five tanks (four Centaurs and one Sherman) landed by 1st RM Armoured Support Regiment, four were knocked out by mines or anti-tank fire.

This photograph was taken at about 1115 hours on D-Day. There are thousands of shell craters around WN-36 and les Roquettes from the run-in shoot by 90th and 147th Field Regiments. Gap 3, quickly opened but then closed by German fire, is 250 metres from WN-36. *LCT 886*, damaged and beached after drifting east from WN-37, can also be seen. *(Keele University Air Photo Archive)*

Key

a. Extreme eastern part of WN-37
b. Lateral minefield
c. Coastal road
d. Gap 3
e. WN-36
f. *LCT 886*
g. Vehicle column
h. Incomplete road (modern D514)

i. Flailed path through minefield
j. Les Roquettes
k. Smoke from burning marsh grasses
l. German trenches
m. Asnelles church
n. 1st Hampshires' battalion headquarters
o. Meuvaines

1st Hampshires' assault companies (A and B) arrived ten minutes after the breaching teams, and were hit by mortar bombs, shells and machine-gun rounds as they disembarked. The fire came mainly from WN-37, but unanticipated problems were also caused by WN-36. This position was supposed to be attacked by 1st Dorsets. However, owing to the strong north-westerly wind and current, its LCAs were pushed east during the run-in and landed a considerable distance away, on Jig Red (as did the remaining three breaching teams). For similar reasons, compounded by a navigational error, 1st Hampshires also landed over half a kilometre from the intended position, on Jig Green East instead of Jig Green West. Although this meant the Hampshires did not have to face short range fire from WN-37, it also meant they had to overcome WN-36 before attempting to fulfil their own tasks.

Quickly, 1st Hampshires' A Company traversed the beach and attacked WN-36. The defenders were still groggy from the preliminary bombardment (which had been both heavy and accurate), and after some close-quarters fighting most were killed or captured. Leaving one platoon to mop up, A Company pushed along the beach towards its objectives in le Hamel, while B Company moved inland towards the farm at les Roquettes, in preparation for a further advance into Asnelles. Meanwhile, 1st Hampshires' C and D Companies, together with battalion headquarters, landed on Jig Green East. Crossing the beach, the commanding officer, Lt-Col H.D. Nelson-Smith, MC, was wounded by a mortar round, and then injured again soon afterwards. C Company's commander, Major David Warren, took over the battalion pending the arrival of 1st Hampshires' second-in-command, Major Charles Martin. However, when Martin landed at H+120 (0925 hours) he was killed instantly. Major Warren commanded 1st Hampshires for the rest of D-Day, service for which he was later awarded the DSO.

Major R.B. Gosling, 147th Field Regiment, RA, was attached to 1st Hampshires' headquarters, which disembarked at about 0745 hours.

An early morning view of Jig Green West, taken from WN-36. In 1944 the top half of the beach was covered with obstacles. Barely visible to the left of the sand coloured tower is WN-37's main casemate, which mounted a 75-mm gun. (Author)

'When the assault companies went in, our own run-in shoot and the rockets had finished and the naval bombardment had lifted, so the beaches suddenly appeared relatively quiet and empty. As we moved into shallow water, however, a swarm of angry bees buzzed just above our heads; our Hampshire comrades, war-experienced, recognized German heavy machine-gun fire and ran forward. In front of us the sand furrowed and spurted from Spandaus firing down the beaches in enfilade on fixed lines from Le Hamel. The colonel shouted for us to lie down, but the wet sand was unattractive, so we sprinted for the cover of the dunes fifty yards ahead.

Some mortar bombs and 88-mm shells were falling and one of the former landed just behind Lieutenant Colonel Nelson-Smith and me, smashing one of his arms and filling my left leg with fragments. We managed to make it to the dunes and flung ourselves in a depression in the sand. Intermittent bombs and shells continued to fall and the bees swarmed through the reeds above our heads. We laid very flat and still.'

Source: Russell Miller, *Nothing less than Victory: the Oral History of D-Day*, p. 351.

A Company's attack on WN-37 (which was supported by part of C Company) went badly. The company commander, Major Richard Baines, was killed while leading his men forward, and most of the other officers and senior NCOs also became casualties. Unfortunately, radio connections with the Navy had temporarily broken down. Consequently, although limited assistance was provided by the destroyer HMS *Undine* and by *LCS(L) 251*, which engaged WN-37 at point-blank range until the recoil cylinder on its 6-pounder gun broke, it proved impossible to elicit any significant naval gunfire support until the late afternoon, after the position had fallen. Furthermore, when the DDs of B Squadron, Sherwood Rangers, disembarked at 0800 hours, three tanks drowned, others were knocked out and most of the remainder became stuck on or near the beach. Three Churchill Crocodile flame-thrower tanks, which had been allocated to 1st Hampshires for their attack on le Hamel and Asnelles, also drowned while attempting to land at the same time.

Deciding that a frontal attack on WN-37 was impossible, Major Warren directed that the attempt be abandoned and another assault mounted from its landward side. Withdrawing A Company's survivors, he amalgamated them with C Company and sent them inland after B Company, which had already left for Asnelles. By late morning the joint C/A Company was advancing towards Asnelles via les Roquettes. Although movement was hampered by the presence of numerous minefields (many of which were actually dummies), little resistance was encountered and C/A Company entered Asnelles at about midday.

The view across the marshes behind Jig Green East. About 1.5 km away a yellow field and a small wood can be seen. On D-Day this area was held by elements of 3/ Ost 441, ideally placed to fire on the troops landing on Jig sector. *(Author)*

STAND B2: ASNELLES

DIRECTIONS: From WN-36, walk east into Jig Red sector, where 1st Dorsets' assault companies (A and B) disembarked under heavy fire (only C Company, from the reserve wave, landed in its planned position at WN-36). Use the path along the dunes, which offers excellent views of the Meuvaines ridge. You can also see the old coast road (now closed), which runs parallel with the seafront 100 metres from it, and which was heavily used by traffic attempting to move inland on D-Day. Jig Red extends as far as WN-35, which is visited in Tour A (Stand A2).

Unfortunately there is no identifiable evidence of a small position stormed by the Dorsets' B Company in the middle of Jig Red, approximately 1 km east of WN-36. As you walk east (it is up to you how far you go), look across the marshes to your right; slightly surprisingly, 1st Dorsets' B Company chose to move through this area to its objective at les Roquettes, 1 km away. It took almost two hours to make the trip. Having reached les Roquettes, B Company remained there for most of the rest of D-Day, ready to defend this critical beach exit against German counter-attacks. The rest of 1st Dorsets advanced inland some time after 0900 hours, followed by 2nd Devons. Most of this battalion had been pushed onto Jig Green East and Jig Red by the wind and current, but got safely ashore by about 0830 hours.

Return to the car park and drive back to the D514 via les Roquettes. Go straight ahead (south) at the crossroads along a minor road, signposted to Meuvaines. From here you can get a good view of the valley of la Gronde Ruisseau, down which 2nd Devons advanced towards Ryes in the late morning. After 1 km take a sharp right turn onto the D65a. This brings you into Asnelles roughly where 1st Hampshires' B and C/A Companies entered after attacking across the fields from les Roquettes. Drive slowly, looking to the right for a small red house, site of the Hampshires' battalion headquarters on 6 June.

At the first junction you come to turn left onto the Rue d'Église. Park by the church, which was used by

1st Hampshires (assisted by French nuns and some villagers) as an aid post for wounded soldiers on D-Day.

THE ACTION: After assembling at les Roquettes, at approximately 0915 hours 1st Hampshires' B Company (Major A. Mott) advanced towards Asnelles. As it did so it suffered some casualties from a small position east of the village. Nevertheless, after a short struggle the German trenches were cleared or by-passed and the company entered the village, probably very close to the church. Meanwhile, 1st Dorsets' C Company swung further inland, meeting considerable opposition from the buildings at the southern end of Asnelles. After killing six Germans and capturing ten the company pushed on towards the battalion's objectives on the ridge 2 km to the west.

While B Company consolidated its position, other elements of 1st Hampshires percolated into the village. By midday these included battalion headquarters, C/A Company and elements of the Support Company. Several tanks and self-propelled guns also entered Asnelles, having run the gauntlet past WN-37. One of B Squadron, Sherwood Rangers' DD tanks was knocked out close to 1st Hampshires' battalion headquarters, probably by a gun located near Meuvaines.

During the early afternoon, after the centre of Asnelles had been cleared of its remaining defenders, Major Warren decided to start the attack against WN-37. His plan was for B Company to capture the crossroads 200 metres south

The view from Asnelles church, looking west down the Rue de la Cavée. This part of the village has changed little since 1944. Close-quarters fighting in such an environment is manpower-intensive and time-consuming. *(Author)*

The red house,
Asnelles, site of
1st Hampshires'
battalion
headquarters.
The road at
the right of the
photograph,
which is taken
looking south-
east, is the D65a.
(Author)

of the western end of WN-37 (now the Place Alexander Stanier), while C/A Company advanced north to the main coastal road (now Rue The Devonshire Regiment) on B Company's right flank. C/A Company would then provide covering fire as B Company assaulted WN-37. Following a report from B Company that it held the crossroads, at 1345 hours C/A Company's advance began. After an hour, during which a dozen Germans were captured and others killed, it reached its allocated positions.

STAND B3: WIDERSTANDSNEST 37

DIRECTIONS: Retrace your route to the previous road junction and bear left towards the coast. After 20 metres, turn left again onto the Rue Paul Helaine. This was the axis followed by the Hampshires' B Company, with C/A Company advancing to its right through an area that was mostly fields in 1944, but which has subsequently become more built-up. Follow the Rue Paul Helaine as it bends right, past the *mairie* (town hall) to the D514 crossroads. This is the Place Alexander Stanier, named after 231st Brigade's commander. Thirty metres away, north-east of the D514, there is a memorial to 2nd South Wales Borderers, who passed through Asnelles on D-Day as part of 56th Brigade. Slightly further east, at the entrance to the Rue The Devonshire Regiment (the western end of the old coast road) there is a memorial to 231st Brigade. Facilities at the Place Alexander Stanier include an information board, shops and restaurants.

The Rue de Southampton, along which B Company advanced from the crossroads to WN-37. The Château Asnelles, which was outside WN-37's perimeter, is visible in the centre, between the smaller houses west of the road. The houses provided critical cover for B Company's attack. *(Author)*

From the Place Alexander Stanier, continue towards the seafront along the Rue de Southampton as far as Asnelles château *(above)*. Again, this was the route followed by 1st Hampshires' B Company (now at less than half strength, and with all three of its platoon commanders dead or dying) as it closed with WN-37. Turn right onto the Rue Xavier D'Anselm and continue 150 metres to a car park.

Since the war this area has been re-developed, and no trace survives of the sanatorium that lay at the heart of WN-37 on D-Day. Nevertheless, here you will find one of

The heavily damaged 75-mm gun casemate at WN-37. The roof of the coastguard tower, built on a German emplacement, is visible over the casemate's rear. Although a plaque credits this position's destruction to a 147th Field Regiment self-propelled gun, it was not completely neutralised until attacked by Lance-Sergeant Scaife's AVRE. Even then, some sources suggest it was used by German snipers until cleared by a patrol from 6th Border Regiment, the Jig sector beach battalion, later on D-Day. *(Author)*

the most important relics of the struggle for le Hamel. This is the battle-scarred 75-mm gun casemate shown on p.143. Next to it there is a position built into the sea wall, and at the eastern end of the car park there is a 'Tobruk' (a type of small concrete underground shelter, usually mounting a machine gun or mortar). The 75-mm gun casemate displays a plaque honouring the role of 147th Field Regiment (which landed nearby as part of 8th Armoured Brigade) in the north-west European campaign.

THE ACTION: After 1st Hampshires failed to capture WN-37 at the start of the day, little progress was made towards the position from the east. At approximately 0930 hours 2nd Devons' C Company approached the strongpoint, *en route* to its battalion assembly area in Asnelles. Having got within 30 metres of the defences it lost its commander, killed by a German sniper. Pinned down by the enemy's fire, C Company remained stuck near WN-37 for most of D-Day.

An unidentified 1st Hampshires' medic recalled the fighting for WN-37.

'Around what was probably noon, I was finally creeping up a road, screened by a self-propelled gun. There were many dead Hampshires along the road, so there was no doubting the direction. Many of these had been inflicted from a heavily fortified sanatorium, which had accounted for several tanks. Its main armament was by now silent, but some of its machine guns [were] still active. The SP by which I was crouching opened up at the sanatorium and nearly deafened me. As I cringed, someone waved at me from the wayside ditch. I stooped to speak to him as a line of machine gun bullets wanged on the armour where I had been seconds before. In it [the ditch] was one of our stretcher bearers with a wounded man. Dragging, crawling and crouching we carried the man back to a large captured bunker, being used as a dressing station. I was by then too exhausted and scared to go back up the road. The other man felt the same.'

Source: Personal account held in the Royal Hampshire Regiment Museum, Winchester.

WN-37 was eventually overrun between about 1500 and 1700 hours. Sources are confused and contradictory, with several units (and individuals) claiming complete or partial credit for its capture. However, it seems likely that the leading role was played by about 50 men from 1st Hampshires' B Company. An invaluable contribution was also made by a single 82nd Assault Squadron AVRE commanded by Lance-Sergeant Scaife, which fired at least two petard rounds into the sanatorium at the heart of the position, breaking the defenders' morale and prompting their surrender. The AVRE then moved east, discharging another round into the rear of the 75-mm gun casemate 50 metres away and prompting a general capitulation among the surviving defenders. About 30 prisoners were taken.

With WN-37 finally neutralised, Jig Green was opened to uninterrupted work by the obstacle demolition teams, assisted by German prisoners. By 1900 hours the eastern sector had been almost cleared, while good progress was made on Jig Green West. During the evening work also began on Item Red, which extended along le Hamel seafront, and from which several ramps led into the village, and thence to roads heading inland.

STAND B4: WIDERSTANDSNEST 38

DIRECTIONS: Walk west along the seafront, either via the Boulevard de la Mer and the coastal path, or along the beach (*see top photo p. 22*). After 750 metres you will reach a well-preserved gun emplacement. In 1944 this was part of WN-38, a platoon position at the western end of le Hamel. The main purpose of this *Widerstandsnest* was to protect the beaches to the east and west, from which a potentially useful exit road ran south through le Carrefour (marked on 1944 maps as St-Côme-de-Fresne).

WN-38's
50-mm anti-tank
gun position.
Although the gun
could fire along
an extensive
section of the
coast, it could
not do so
against Jig Beach.
Arromanches
is just visible in
the dip in the
cliffs beyond the
emplacement,
while WN-39 is
located on the
slopes to the left.
(Author)

THE ACTION: After the fall of WN-37, WN-38 was attacked by 1st Hampshires' C/A Company, supported by Lance-Sergeant Scaife's AVRE. Although the defenders fought hard, they had no answer to the AVRE, which blasted their positions in the fortified houses to pieces. Following a brief but furious action, 20 more Germans surrendered.

STAND B5: WIDERSTANDSNEST 39

DIRECTIONS: Return to your vehicle and drive back to the D514. Turn right (west) towards Arromanches. Exit Asnelles and continue for 750 metres. Pass the church at la Fontaine St-Côme on your left and head uphill. After 100 metres, turn left onto a side road. This loops briefly before turning back uphill. Look to your right for a concrete casemate, part of WN-39. Park safely and look back towards Asnelles.

THE ACTION: Although fighting continued in Asnelles for most of D-Day, considerable numbers of British troops were able to avoid the village and advance towards their own objectives. These included 1st Dorsets, which captured the high ground south of Arromanches (Point 54, plus the positions at WN-40 and WN-41) during the afternoon; 2nd Devons, which took Ryes at 1630 hours; and 56th Brigade, which began its advance towards Bayeux in the early evening.

Among the forces that by-passed Asnelles was 1st Hampshires' D Company, commanded by Major John Littlejohns. Its objective was the capture of the two casemates at WN-39. These were hit by the Dutch gunboat *Flores* at the start of the day, but because their embrasures faced almost due east and could not be struck frontally from the sea, the shelling had little effect. Despite frequent resumptions of the bombardment, WN-39 continued to fire on the beaches into the early afternoon.

WN-39 was finally attacked at about 1500 hours by Major Littlejohns' men, assisted by several tanks, probably from B Squadron, Sherwood Rangers. Some casualties were taken crossing the open ground to the south-east, but resistance within WN-39 was negligible and D Company quickly rounded up over 30 prisoners (XXX Corps' signal log reported the position captured at 1520 hours). The guns themselves were destroyed by 73rd Field Company on 8 June, using demolition charges.

STAND B6: STÜTZPUNKT ARROMANCHES

DIRECTIONS: Follow the side road until it rejoins the D514. Turn left, taking care as the road can be busy. Continue 500 metres before turning right into the car park at *Stützpunkt Arromanches*. Here you will find various relics from the naval radar station that was located here in 1944, plus a viewing platform and a 360-degree cinema. This rather unusual venue shows a 20-minute film called *The Price of Liberty*, which mixes archive and modern footage.

The view from WN-39, looking east over Asnelles and le Hamel. One of its casemates mounted an 88-mm gun, the other, a 75-mm field gun. The latter fired 124 rounds, probably more than any similar weapon defending Gold Beach. WN-36 is 2.5 km away – about the maximum effective range for these guns. *(Author)*

ARROMANCHES 360-DEGREE CINEMA

Arromanches 360, Chemin du Calvaire – BP 9, 14117 Arromanches; tel: +33 (0)2 31 22 30 30; web: <www.arromanches360.com>. Open 0940–1840 daily Jun–Aug; 1010–1740 daily Apr–May, Sept–Oct;1010–1640 Feb, Dec; 1010–1710 March, Nov; closed Jan (two shows per hour when open). Entrance fee.

THE ACTION: According to 1st Hampshires' original plan, *Stützpunkt Arromanches* was to be taken by B and C Companies after they had occupied le Hamel and Asnelles. However, because they were still bogged down in the village, the attack was carried out on Major Warren's orders by D Company (with whom Warren had radio contact) soon after it had captured WN-39. Again, little resistance was met; the strongpoint was manned mainly by naval personnel with little training in ground fighting, and the position fell quickly after a short artillery bombardment and the infantry assault. Forty prisoners were taken.

In the early evening 1st Hampshires consolidated its hold on the cliffs east of Arromanches. Ammunition was replenished, and B and C/A Companies moved forward to join Littlejohns' men. Meanwhile, naval gunfire was brought to bear on Arromanches and the position immediately west of it (WN-44), with the aim of softening up the village's defences before the Hampshires' assault.

The final attack took place at approximately 2000 hours. Many of the defenders had fled, and 1st Hampshires

The concrete base of the *Seeriese* FuMO 214 radar set (a type referred to by the Allies as the 'Giant Würzburg') at *Stützpunkt Arromanches*. (Author)

suffered not a single casualty during this concluding phase of a hard day's battle. Instead, its soldiers entered Arromanches to a rapturous welcome from the local population. By 2100 hours WN-43 and WN-44 had fallen, and the village was secured. A few prisoners (plus a dog which became the Hampshires' mascot) were taken.

The Hampshires' day was over. It had cost them 182 killed and wounded, by some margin the heaviest losses incurred by any of the 15 infantry battalions (including 47 RM Commando and the two beach battalions) that landed on Gold Beach on D-Day.

ENDING THE TOUR: After examining the site of the *Stützpunkt*, walk towards the cliff path at its western end, where a flight of steps leads into Arromanches. Go down to the casemate at WN-43, which has a Sherman tank on top, and which on D-Day mounted a 105-mm mountain gun. In 1944 all the houses between this position and the beach were demolished, so as to provide a clear field of fire (*see lower photo p. 111*).

Continue downhill to visit the excellent D-Day museum on the seafront and – if the tide is out – the dramatic remains of the Mulberry Harbour. Arromanches itself has many hotels, restaurants and shops. It is easy to spend several enjoyable hours here, relaxing after your tour.

Alternatively, you might want to visit the Longues Battery on the cliffs 5 km west of Arromanches. To do so, follow the D514 through Tracy-sur-Mer and Manvieux and turn right at Longues. The site is one of the best preserved coastal batteries in Normandy and access is possible at any time. The capture of Longues is described on p. 89.

D-DAY LANDING MUSEUM

Musée du Débarquement, Place du 6 Juin, 14117 Arromanches; tel: +33 (0)2 31 22 34 31; web: <www.musee-arromanches.fr>. See website for opening hours. Entrance fee.

47 COMMANDO, ESCURES TO PORT-EN-BESSIN

OBJECTIVE: This tour covers the capture of Port-en-Bessin by 47 Royal Marine Commando.

DURATION/SUITABILITY: The tour lasts half a day. The total distance is 7 km, over half of it on foot. Port-en-Bessin has narrow, one-way streets so cyclists are advised to secure bicycles at Stand C2 and undertake the rest of the tour on foot. For those with mobility difficulties, stands C1, C3, C4 and C5 involve steep ascents or descents, in C4's case using steps that become slippery in wet weather. Disabled tourers should allow extra time and consider seeking assistance if they want to undertake this tour.

STARTING THE TOUR: The tour begins at Mont Cavalier, near the village of Escures. Your most likely approach is along the D6 and then through Escures to just north of Mont Cavalier. If you approach from the north-east on the D514, turn onto the D100 at Commes, signposted to Etreham and Tour-en-Bessin, and continue for 1.5 km to Escures.

STAND C1: MONT CAVALIER (POINT 72)

DIRECTIONS: Park in Escures and walk towards the high ground south-east of the village. Access to Mont Cavalier – which in 1944 was known as Point 72 – is via the track entrance shown on p.154. Despite a sign

'WESTERN FEATURE'

Feux

Résurgence
de l'Aure

WN-57

Phr

WN-36

WN-58

Vauban

les Droues

la Goulette

58

62

Port en Bessin

'EASTERN FEATURE'
STÜTZPUNKT
PORT-EN-BESSIN

49

53

37

22

17

le Vignet

P

C2

D514

Ec

Gend

St. épur.

15

Coll.

13

D514

D 514

0.4

C

le Bouffay

LONGUES &
ARROMANCHES

le Lieu Barry

74

D514

le

34

D514

AHA
CH

WN-58

la Prairie

Golf

ssin-Huppain

12

Pyl.

8

15

Commes

66

la Bauquerie

63

68

le Mont

35

D100

D100

Château
du Bosq

68

63

a

Musée

15

17

D 6

15

Escures

20

21

24

24

26

25

26

69

le Mont

30

24

C1

GR de

67

Bne

25

1

25

Baron

Petite

Grippe Sault

29

Mont Cavalier

30

POINT 72 (1944 Maps)

les Allouas

20

Brandel

22

20

le Lieu Aubin

22

les Tourneresses

Perte

15

18

23

D 153

le Petit Argouges

Manoir

la Fosse
du Soucy

17

17

21

Aure Riv.

le Bas Verger

le Pont Fâtu

St. pomp.

le Petit Brandel

22

29

le Moulin Gérard

la vieille Riv.

Bas Maisons
Ferme
du Carel

2

Etot

le Bas Secron
Ec.

l'Orangerie

36

la Ma

35

rgerie

21

24

arrefour
Plate Voie

22

D 153

le Lieu
Picard

21

St. pomp.

la Fosse
Buhot

0,3

C

41

D100

29

la Poste

24

31

Maisons

Hérils

les Goupillaires

le Haut Hérils

40

Ruliercy

les Carrières

le Pèti

To
BAYEUX

<table>
<tr><td>a</td><td>Museum of Underwater Wrecks</td></tr>
<tr><td>①</td><td>47 RM Commando's approximate route to Point 72</td></tr>
<tr><td>②</td><td>Château Maisons (Fosse Soucy); headquarters I/GR 726</td></tr>
<tr><td></td><td>Base map: IGN 1512OT</td></tr>
</table>

0.5

1

Kilometres

warning that Mont Cavalier itself is a private hunting ground (*Chasse Gardée*), the IGN map clearly identifies this as a public footpath. Provided you stay on the track and respect private property, you should encounter no difficulties. Walk 250 metres uphill and look north to Port-en-Bessin. Although you cannot see the harbour (it is 15 metres below the level of the church and 500 metres further north), the dominating heights on either side of it are clearly visible. In 1944 these were referred to by the British as the 'Western Feature' and 'Eastern Feature'. Both were strongly defended.

THE ACTION: Port-en-Bessin was significant to the invasion planners for two reasons. First, it offered a small but sheltered harbour, which could be used for unloading supplies. Second – and more important – the town lay on the boundary between the American and British assault sectors. If a secure connection was to be achieved between the Americans and British, the port had to be taken quickly, before the Germans established a significant presence within an area of potential Allied weakness.

The task of capturing Port-en-Bessin was given to 47 RM Commando, led by Lt-Col C.F. Phillips. This was a well trained unit with a core of experienced soldiers. On D-Day it included a headquarters, a heavy weapons troop (mortars and machine guns), five commando troops (A, B, Q, X and Y) and a carrier section (four light tracked vehicles, carrying extra weapons and ammunition). Each troop comprised 3 officers and 60 men, making it about half the size of an ordinary infantry company. Total strength on D-Day was 420 men.

Phillips recognised the difficulties involved in capturing Port-en-Bessin, which was flanked on both sides by 50–60 metre cliffs, and was known to be well protected against amphibious assault. He therefore decided to attack from the south, over easier terrain. This meant landing on Gold Beach, 13 km away, and making a forced march to the objective. Despite the distance, and the fact that each soldier would be carrying 40 kilograms of equipment, Phillips believed this would give significant advantages. In particular, his men would be able to deploy in an organised fashion before attacking, and could concentrate where the defences were weakest. Provided the enemy was 'softened up' beforehand, Phillips believed that Port-en-Bessin could be taken within five or six hours of the commando's initial landing.

Phillips' plan envisaged four phases:

- In Phase I, 47 RM Commando would land on Jig Green Beach at H+120 (0925 hours), and advance via Asnelles to a forward assembly area at la Rosière, arriving by 1100 hours.

- In Phase II the Commando would move 7 km across country, by-passing opposition to seize Point 72 by 1300 hours. Point 72 provided excellent observation over the surrounding area, and would serve as a 'firm base' for the attack.

- In Phase III, following an air, land and sea bombardment co-ordinated by observers attached to Phillips' headquarters, the commandos would attack the Eastern Feature. Additional support might be available from a US artillery battalion, from Omaha Beach, but in the event this did not materialise. Phase III would begin some time after 1400 hours.

- In Phase IV the Commando would capture the Western Feature and secure the town.

At approximately 0950 hours on 6 June, 47 RM Commando disembarked along a 1.5 km stretch of Jig Beach. Unfortunately, it did so in considerable disarray. One LCA was sunk by enemy fire on the run-in, and four others were destroyed (and seven damaged) when they hit submerged beach obstacles. Many personnel had to swim ashore, and numerous weapons – as well as uniforms, boots and three of the Marines' four radio sets – were lost in the process. Of the commando's 420 soldiers, 76 were killed, wounded or missing. Among the latter was Lt-Col Phillips, who reached the beach safely, but who was temporarily unable to locate his men.

Above: The
entrance to
Mont Cavalier,
Escures. As
the spot height
on the map
shows, the ridge
(visible behind
the buildings)
is 64 metres
above sea level.
In accordance
with wartime
usage, however,
the feature is
referred to here
as Point 72.
(Author)

In the absence of their CO, the commandos were
rallied by the unit's second-in-command, Major P.M.
Donnell. This took two hours, during which weapons
and ammunition were collected from any available
source (including British and German casualties), but by
midday 47 RM Commando was ready to advance inland.
Skirting the fighting at Asnelles, it reached the Meuvaines–
le Carrefour road at 1400 hours, where it was joined by
Phillips and a few others. The Commando, by now about
360 strong, then moved west towards its objective.

After several encounters with small groups of Germans,
including a sharp fight at la Rosière that caused further
delay, the commandos reached Point 72 at last light
(2230 hours). Since it was too late to attack that day, and
conscious of the need to re-organise, Phillips ordered his men
to dig in on the ridge. Patrols were also sent into Escures,
where a German medical bunker was discovered. From
one of its personnel it was learned that enemy forces were
nearby. These were elements of 726th Grenadier Regiment's
1st Battalion (I/GR 726), the headquarters of which was in
the Château Maisons 800 metres south of Mont Cavalier.

During the morning of 7 June, 47 RM Commando
prepared to launch its assault. Its remaining radio was
repaired, and arrangements were made for a one-hour
bombardment of Port-en-Bessin (especially the Eastern
Feature). This would start at 1500 hours, carried out by the
cruiser HMS *Emerald* (seven 6-inch guns) and two LCG(L)s
(each with two 4.7-inch guns). Just before the attack RAF

Opposite: The
view from Mont
Cavalier. Port-en-
Bessin church is
clearly visible, as
are the Western
and Eastern
Features. (Author)

Typhoons would strafe the defences, while 431st Battery, 147th Field Regiment, laid down a smoke screen to cover the Commando's advance. The attack itself would begin at 1600 hours. Phillips' plan was for X Troop to capture the small strongpoint south-west of the town (WN-58), while A and B Troops moved through Port-en-Bessin to attack the Western and Eastern features respectively. A tactical headquarters under Major Donnell would accompany the assault force, although Lt-Col Phillips himself would remain at Point 72. Q Troop, severely under strength after its D-Day losses, would be in reserve at Escures, as was the Heavy Weapons Troop. Y Troop – also depleted and short of weapons – was to defend the firm base and rear headquarters on Mont Cavalier against any attack from the direction of Château Maisons.

At 1500 hours, as the bombardment began, the assault groups set off through Escures. The route towards their objectives was along the main road into Port-en-Bessin.

Above: To minimise the chances of meeting the enemy, 47 RM Commando's route to Point 72 took it across country and along minor roads like this one, from la Buhennerie to le Mont. Note the hedges, and the way in which the road bend restricts visibility to barely a hundred metres. *(Author)*

STAND C2:
PORT-EN-BESSIN CHURCH

DIRECTIONS: Return to your vehicle and join the D6 at Escures. Drive north for 1 km, following the Marines' axis of advance. Note the high ground to your front left, which is now a golf course, but which in 1944 was the site of WN-58. When you reach the roundabout on the town's southern outskirts, ignore the *Toutes Directions* ('all routes') sign and continue straight ahead for 500 metres to the D514 crossroads. After another 150 metres, park near the church on your right.

THE ACTION: Despite harassing fire, X, A and B Troops reached the outskirts of Port-en-Bessin by 1600 hours. Guided by a local *gendarme*, Henri George Gouget, A and B Troops continued north, using ditches to conceal their movement. On reaching the main coast road (D514) they split into two. A Troop moved north-west along the Rue Nationale towards the harbour and the Western Feature. Simultaneously, Captain Isherwood's B Troop advanced towards the inner basin and the Eastern Feature. By now the supporting bombardment had lifted, although clouds of smoke still obscured visibility, especially around the Eastern Feature, where grass fires continued to burn after HMS *Emerald*'s shelling.

While A and B Troops entered the town, Captain Walton's X Troop approached WN-58, closing behind the hedges west of the main road to within 200 metres of the position. Led by their commander, two sections charged forward, bayonets fixed and guns firing, with the men yelling at the tops of their voices. Despite their fortifications, the Germans surrendered immediately, their will to fight broken by the terrifying figures only a short distance away. Having mopped up the strongpoint, X Troop then advanced north, following A Troop towards the north-west end of the basin.

STAND C3: THE WESTERN FEATURE

DIRECTIONS: Before leaving Stand C2, look at the interesting and moving memorial by the church. This identifies 21 citizens of Port-en-Bessin who perished in the war, among them 11 killed during the town's liberation. Perhaps most poignantly, the memorial also lists the names of 18 fishermen who died between December 1944 and August 1948 when their boats struck sea mines. They include four members of one family and three from another.

Cross the road and head south for a few metres to a side road with a 'no vehicular access' sign at its entrance. This is the Rue Nationale, along which Captain T.F. Cousins' A Troop advanced towards its objective. Walk down this road towards the seafront. After approximately 300 metres, note the courtyards and alleys to your left. These provided hiding places for the soldiers of both sides on 7 June, and represented a complicating factor in the struggle for Port-en-Bessin.

Continue to the junction shown below. Turn left along the Rue Traversière to the T-junction with the Rue du Nord. Turn right, and after a few metres turn left up the steep, cobbled Rue du Phare. Again, this is the route followed by A Troop. Despite the fact that German patrols were roaming the town's streets, A Troop reached this point without encountering any resistance.

Head (slowly!) uphill, passing the 'Lady of the Harbour' lighthouse after 250 metres. Look left for views of Mont Cavalier, Escures and the site of WN-58. At the top, turn right past a golf course sand bunker to the cliff edge, where there is a set of steps into a German pillbox, built into the cliff. Part of this position is sealed, but access to the rest may still be possible.

You are now well within the perimeter of the Western Feature (WN-57), which stretched down the cliff face and terraces to the quay below. In 1944 the position was surrounded by barbed wire and mines, with a wire entanglement across the Rue du Phare. It contained about a platoon of soldiers from *Hauptmann* (Captain) Hiesekorn's 1st Company, I/GR 726. Together with the

a 'Lady of the Harbour' lighthouse
b Southern end of inner basin in June 1944
c Zig-zag path
① Position of German artillery barges, midday 6 June

Base map: IGN 1512OT

To
ESCURES &
BAYEUX

To
OMAHA
BEACH

'WESTERN FEATURE'
WN-57

WN-56

Tour Vauban

EASTERN FEATURE

Port en Bessin

Feux

Résurgence
de l'Aure

Phare

WN-58

la Prairie

Huppain

Gend.

St. épur.

Pyl.

LONGUE
ARROMANCHE

D514

D514

D6

0   250   5
Metres

The junction between the Rue Nationale and the Rue Michel le Fournier (beyond the 'no entry' sign). The Rue Traversière is to the left, next to the fishing shop. The complex layout of the old town made it difficult to secure. According to civilian eyewitness accounts, soldiers from both sides sometimes passed within metres of one another without being aware of their opponents' presence. *(Author)*

rest of the company (on the Eastern Feature), and around 100 sailors from three artillery barges of the 6. *Artillerie-trägerflottille* based in Port-en-Bessin, they were the town's principal defenders.

THE ACTION: A Troop's attack on the Western Feature began at about 1630 hours, and initially progressed satisfactorily. Under the direction of Lieutenant Goldstein, a bangalore torpedo (a tubular explosive device designed to cut barbed wire) was inserted through the roadblock on the Rue du Phare and detonated. A Troop then passed through the gap, dividing into two groups of roughly 30 men apiece. Lieutenant Goldstein led one party to the left, to attack the strongpoint from the south-east, while Lieutenant Wilson took the other to the right to deal with the positions overlooking the harbour.

Below: The view from the bottom of the Rue du Phare, looking up towards the Western Feature. The barbed wire entanglement across the road was beyond the house (only partly visible) furthest from the camera. *(Author)*

This aerial photo of Port-en-Bessin was taken before D-Day. Comparison with
the tour map shows changes since 1944, notably the extended basin. *(IWM CL11)*

Key

a. WN-57 (Western Feature)

b. WN-56 (basin entrance defences)

c. *Stützpunkt Port-en-Bessin* (Eastern
   Feature)

d. WN-58

e. Port-en-Bessin church

f. Graveyard

g. Zig-zag path

h. Site of modern roundabout

i. To Escures [note arrow]

As the commandos emerged onto the open slopes around WN-57, they were hit by a murderous fire. Some was directed from above, but much of it came from the east. As you will see at Stand C4, the Eastern Feature offered excellent views of the top of the Rue du Phare and WN-57. As the smoke cleared, it became possible for the Germans east of the basin to support their comrades half a kilometre away by shooting into A Troop's rear. Additional fire came from at least one of the artillery barges in the harbour. Although German reports indicate these were sunk on 6 June, there is evidence that some of their armament remained operational the following day. This included large calibre automatic cannon and artillery pieces – weapons against which A Troop had no protection.

Within a few minutes Lieutenant Wilson's group was almost wiped out, while Goldstein's men also suffered losses (of some 60 attackers, 11 were killed, 17 wounded and 1 was captured). Captain Cousins had no choice but to order an immediate withdrawal. While many of the wounded commandos took refuge in the houses near the bottom of the Rue du Phare (where they were hidden by French civilians), the remnants of A Troop fell back several hundred metres to regroup. As they did so, they passed through X Troop, which was clearing buildings in the town. The attack on the Western Feature, however, had failed.

A Universal Carrier disembarks alongside the harbour jetty, 10 June 1944. WN-57's cliff-top pillbox is visible on the right of the photo. The four buildings nearest the camera survive today, as does the 'Lady of the Harbour' lighthouse (just visible as the highest man-made structure on the left). *(IWM B5393)*

47 RM Commando's medical officer described the capture of Corporal Amos on the slopes of the Western Feature.

'As the others were withdrawing from the Western Feature, Corporal Amos delayed to apply a field dressing to his troop sergeant, Sergeant Fletcher, who was lying mortally wounded. As Amos finished doing this, he suddenly saw a German above him. The German threw a grenade which exploded beside him, miraculously without seriously injuring him although it tore off part of his trouser leg and left him dazed. As he lay he felt himself being pushed by a foot and turned to find the German standing over him. The German had thought that he was dead. Amos was taken prisoner and, outside one of the strongpoints, was put in charge of a guard who kept his rifle pushed against Amos' temple. Taken later into the strongpoint, he was marched along a trench and into another strongpoint where he was interrogated in front of a notice which said that all captured commandos were to be shot.'

Source: J. Forfar, *From Omaha to the Scheldt: the Story of 47 Royal Marine Commando*, p. 75.

The view from the Western Feature, showing the Eastern Feature and part of the harbour. For protection against amphibious assault, the cliffs in the middle distance had 11-inch naval shells suspended from them, attached to tripwires. The concrete paving in the foreground marks the location of part of the German defences. *(Author)*

STAND C4: THE EASTERN FEATURE

DIRECTIONS: Retrace your steps down the Rue du Phare. Near the bottom, turn left along the Rue de la Croix and continue to the T-junction with the Rue Torteron. To see more of WN-57 or to use the picnic area overlooking the seafront, turn left for 150 metres. Alternatively, continue downhill to the harbour. Here, turn right and walk to the bridge at the basin entrance. If you want a break there are several restaurants here.

Cross the bridge and walk 150 metres across a car park to the concrete blockhouse immediately beneath the round Vauban tower, built in 1694 and taking its name from the famous French fortress architect. Attached to the blockhouse there is a small memorial plaque to 47 RM Commando, and

Port-en-Bessin, then and now. In the 1944 photo note the basin entrance (left, with an anti-tank wall to its right), the *Hôtel de la Marine* (just visible, right) and the German artillery barge in the foreground. (IWM B5395/ Author)

to the Free French cruisers *Georges Leygues* and *Montcalm*. The structure itself was part of WN-56, which protected the harbour area and basin against an amphibious assault. In 1944 it had an obsolete French FT17 tank turret on its roof; this is no longer present.

Walk back across the car park and continue uphill, taking the steps past the tower to the top. Here you will find a concrete emplacement, part of the Eastern Feature. On D-Day this was protected by extensive minefields and wire entanglements, and included deep bunkers, pillboxes, trenches and gun emplacements, together accommodating mortars, machine guns and several larger weapons. From here the Germans dominated much of the town and basin area, and could easily observe activity on Mont Cavalier, 2 km to the south. If you have binoculars, look along the coast to the west for an excellent view of the western part of Omaha Beach, roughly 10 km away.

THE ACTION: According to Phillips' original plan, the Eastern Feature was to be captured before the Western Feature. However, the German position east of the harbour was even stronger than that to the west, and by the time B Troop secured the bottom end of the basin (taking 12 prisoners) its defenders were fully prepared. As well as supporting the garrison of WN-57, the Germans on the Eastern Feature brought down a heavy fire towards the south. Having suffered more than a dozen casualties, B Troop was forced to take cover in buildings in the south-east part of the town.

By the late afternoon, despite some success in clearing the old town, it appeared that 47 RM Commando's attack had stalled. Reinforcements were therefore despatched from Escures, among them Q Troop and the Heavy Weapons Troop. Soon after, Lt-Col Phillips moved into the town to be closer to the action. At about 2100 hours approximately ten carriers under the command of the Marines' Lieutenant Bennett also arrived, having made a daring trip through disputed territory from la Rosière to Escures. Many of these vehicles were manned by soldiers from 2nd Devons, which was advancing along the coast from the east, and whose carrier platoon was placed at Bennett's disposal that morning. They brought with them welcome supplies of ammunition, plus several heavy weapons. With these Phillips hoped to renew the attack on the defences of Port-en-Bessin later that evening.

The protection of the rear headquarters on Point 72 had been seriously weakened by the despatch of the forces mentioned above, and at about 2200 hours it was overrun by a German attack from the direction of Château Maisons. Several Marines were captured, although Y Troop managed to disengage and reach British lines to the east. Despite probing to the outskirts of Port-en-Bessin, however, the Germans were too few to confront the main body of 47 RM Commando, and withdrew south. Escures, Point 72 and the Château Maisons were subsequently secured by 2nd Devons on 8 June.

STAND C5: THE ZIG-ZAG PATH

DIRECTIONS: Before leaving the Eastern Feature, look at the harbour. Note the inner moles, which divide the harbour much more obviously than was the case in 1944. From the tour map it is easy to locate the positions occupied by the German artillery barges. During the late evening of 7 June these were attacked by naval personnel from two destroyers, the Royal Navy's HMS *Ursa* and the Polish vessel *Krakowiak*, which had been lying off Port-en-Bessin since the afternoon. Entering the harbour in two motor boats at approximately 2235 hours, their assault parties boarded two of the barges, but found them unoccupied apart from a few dead sailors and a live dog.

From the cliff edge, walk south-east along the hilltop track towards a water tank 250 metres away. As you do so, look down the slopes to your right, from which 411 mines were lifted by engineers from 73rd Field Company a few days after the town's capture. Sadly, six men were killed and four wounded during these clearance operations. When you reach the water tank, you will see a zig-zag path

The zig-zag path (*foreground*), with Mont Cavalier at top left. *(Author)*

immediately below you. You can also see the bottom end of the modern basin; note that this is a post-war extension, and that in 1944 this area was covered with buildings.

THE ACTION: At about 2000 hours, A and B Troops both sent small parties from the basin area to reconnoitre the approaches to the Eastern Feature. Despite losses to mortar fire, they cleared several buildings at the south-east end of the basin (these survive, but are hidden by the trees between the path and the basin) and headed uphill. Here they discovered a zig-zag path that appeared to lead through the German defences. Led by A Troop's Captain Cousins, the Marines moved up it but then came under fire as they approached the top and withdrew to seek reinforcements.

Having convinced Lt-Col Phillips that the Eastern Feature's perimeter might be penetrated at this point, at 2200 hours Captain Cousins led three officers and 24 Marines back up the zig-zag path. They were supported by covering fire and smoke bombs from the Heavy Weapons Troop and Bennett's carriers, located near the cemetery 400 metres to the south-west. On reaching the top of the path, Cousins fired a red Verey light. This was the signal for the assault force to divide into two, and for its attack to begin. Led by Captain Cousins and Lieutenant Wilson, one party rushed towards the western end of the strongpoint, firing as it went. Meanwhile Captain J.T. Vincent and Lieutenant Stickings (Q Troop) took the other group towards the right, to deal with the German positions on the other half of the feature.

Although the defenders almost certainly outnumbered Cousins' men by four to one, the arrival within their position of a highly aggressive group of Marines appears to have thrown the Germans into consternation. Furthermore, in the twilight it may have seemed that the commandos were far more numerous than they actually were, not least since they attacked in two directions simultaneously. After a flurry of resistance, during which Captain Cousins was killed, the defenders' fighting spirit collapsed. By 2300 hours the Eastern Feature, along with around a hundred prisoners, was in British hands.

The Marines' medical officer described Cousins' death and its effect on the battle.

'Nearing the west end of the hill, [Cousins'] group came under heavy fire from a concrete blockhouse at close range. Cousins halted his men and told them to get into some unoccupied trenches. Taking his Bren gunner, Marine Delap, and Marines Howe, Madden and Tomlinson with him, Cousins led this group through a gap in the wire fence ahead and rushed the blockhouse. All were shooting as they went. As they charged the blockhouse, grenades were thrown at them, and as one exploded in front of him Cousins fell forward, killed outright. Madden received a severe head wound and Delap was concussed. The waiting group under Lt. Wilson... then ran forward as planned... Delap had recovered quickly and was continuing to fire his Bren gun; Tomlinson and Howe were firing and throwing grenades. Wilson by this time had a German prisoner with him who was ordered to shout to the men in the blockhouse to surrender: a white flag appeared and they did so. Cousins had been killed but his sacrifice was not in vain. The blockhouse had not only been captured but its capture and the manner in which this was achieved had weakened enemy morale.'

Source: J. Forfar, *From Omaha to the Scheldt: the Story of 47 Royal Marine Commando,* p. 86.

Watching from nearby, the defenders of WN-57 must have been aware, within a short time, of the fall of the Eastern Feature, and possibly also of the boarding of the artillery barges. Aware, too, that any renewed attack on their position would take place in circumstances very different from those of a few hours earlier, they decided to capitulate. Rather to the commandos' surprise – for they anticipated another bloody battle for the Western Feature – as dawn broke on 8 June, Corporal Amos led 23 Germans down into the town to surrender. Shortly afterwards the Western Feature was occupied by the British. There was no opposition. The battle for Port-en-Bessin was over.

ENDING THE TOUR: Walk down the zig-zag path, pausing to look back up when you reach the bottom. On entering a residential road, continue downhill, taking the gravel track on your right. This leads to the south-eastern corner of the basin. From here, you can look around Port-en-Bessin or, if you prefer to return to your car immediately, walk 200 metres south to the D514 and turn right, passing the cemetery south of the main road before reaching the crossroads near the church. The local tourist office (tel: +33 (0)2 31 21 92 33) is at the crossroads.

From Port-en-Bessin it is only a 15-minute drive down the D6 to the centre of Bayeux (*see p. 110–11*). Alternatively, you might want to visit the D-Day wrecks museum 1 km south of Port-en-Bessin. This contains numerous items salvaged during the 1970s from the waters off Lower Normandy, including tanks and other equipment, as well as a variety of other interesting exhibits.

MUSEUM OF UNDERWATER WRECKS

Musée des Épaves, Route de Bayeux – BP 9, 14520 Port-en-Bessin; tel: +33 (0)2 31 21 17 06. Open 1000–1200 & 1400–1800 weekends only May, 1000–1200 & 1400–1800 daily June & Sept, 1000–1800 daily July & Aug, closed Oct–Apr. Entrance fee.

SAINT-PIERRE

OBJECTIVE: This tour covers the battle for the village of
St-Pierre between 9 and 11 June 1944.

DURATION/SUITABILITY: The tour lasts half a day. The
total distance is 8 km (from Stand D1), one quarter of it
on foot. The tour is through rolling countryside and along
generally quiet roads, and is therefore suitable for cyclists.
For those with mobility difficulties, all stands are accessible
by car. The walking tour at St-Pierre involves one short but
fairly steep ascent.

STARTING THE TOUR: The tour begins in open country
near the village of Audrieu. The best approach is along the
N13 Bayeux–Caen highway. Turn off by the water tower
1.5 km east of St-Léger, heading south on the D158b, which
meets the D158 at Loucelles. In June 1944 this was 8th
Armoured Brigade's 'Route Congo'. Cross the railway at le
Bas d'Audrieu on the D158 and join the D82 at Audrieu.
Continue south, pausing to visit the battle-scarred Église
Notre Dame on the right. Almost opposite the church there
is a small plaque commemorating the commune's liberation
by 1st Dorsets (see pp. 96–7). A few metres further south,
in a lay-by, there is a sombre reminder of the savagery with
which the Normandy fighting was sometimes conducted.
This is a memorial listing the names of 64 Canadian soldiers
who were murdered in captivity by 12th SS Panzer Division
between 8 and 11 June 1944. Of these, 24 were shot in the
grounds of the Château d'Audrieu, visible 300 metres away.

Approximately 200 metres south of the church, turn right
onto the D178. Drive 800 metres to the junction with the road
to Hervieu and park on the grass verge. This is Stand D1.

To
BAYEUX

St-Léger

a Woods from which Sherwood Rangers
  advanced to Point 103, 8 June
b Bayeux–Caen railway
c Église Notre Dame
d Château d'Audrieu
  Base map: IGN 1512OT

N13

le Parc

Carcagny

Chât.
d'eau

les Crottes

la Rivière

le Silo

CA

Champ Briseuille

Vieille Terre

C 0,15

Ducy-Ste-Marguerite

D 82

Épine Mauget

le Lombois

Pont de Condé

sur-Seulles

le Moulin

Loucel

Mon.

les Fontaines

le Raimbault

Palli

le Château

a

D 158

la Cour d'Enfer

Lieu Moussard

b

Arrêt

St. épur

D 187

le Haut des Jardins

le Bas
d'Audrieu

la Mar

le Bas du Désert

Hervieu

Ferme
de la Motte

le Calvaire

le Jardin Barbier

la Fosse Touraille

Audrieu

Ferme du Petit Val

le Mouton

C 0,9

D 82

Ferme
de la Rue Jugan

D1

D 178

c

Éc.

le Moulin
de Taillebosq

la Sente Cornet

Motte
féodale

d

le Château

le Grand Champ

Hameau Pavie

Ferme du Thuit

Ferme du Pont Roch

les Vallées

Ferme d'Apremont

le Haut
d'Audrieu

Ferme de la Croix

C 0,15

Cristot

les Longs Champs

Chât. d'eau

la Ferme Bellemare

0   0.5   1

Kilometres

POINT 103
(1944 Maps)

To
ST-PIERRE

les Blochères

Above: The Canadian memorial, Audrieu. The Château d'Audrieu, where Canadian and British prisoners were murdered by SS troops, is in the background. *(Author)*

STAND D1:
THE ADVANCE TO POINT 103

DIRECTIONS: From Stand D1 you have excellent views over countryside that has changed very little since 1944. Note in particular the woods near Ducy-Ste-Marguerite (due north), from which the tanks of the Sherwood Rangers advanced to capture Point 103 on 8 June (*see p. 96*). Note also the Église Notre Dame to the east and the Seulles valley to the west. Looking south, you can see the ground sloping up to a concrete water tower, to the right of which is Point 103.

THE ACTION: By the evening of 8 June, Brigadier Cracroft's 8th Armoured Brigade had made limited progress towards Villers-Bocage. Nevertheless, its troops had taken Loucelles

Below: The view from Stand D1, looking south. Point 103 is on the left, beyond the yellow crops (note the water tower). This is almost exactly the view that 8th DLI's soldiers would have had during the morning of 9 June. *(Author)*

This photograph
shows the superb
views looking
south from Point
103. The road
is the D82. 8th
DLI's C and
D Companies
advanced across
the fields shown
here during the
late afternoon of
9 June, protected
by 24th Lancers'
C Squadron.
(Author)

and parts of le Bas d'Audrieu and Audrieu, and seized
high ground at Point 103. During the night of 8–9 June
two machine-gun platoons and an anti-tank battery were
sent to secure this critical feature. Two Sherwood Rangers
officers also scouted St-Pierre, which lay astride the
brigade's intended axis of advance 1.5 km south of Point
103. Encountering German troops, they returned to report
the village held by the enemy.

Brigadier Cracroft decided he needed more infantry
to capture St-Pierre and occupy the ridge 3 km south of
it (the 'Tessel–Bretteville Feature'). Late on 8 June the
8th Battalion, Durham Light Infantry, (8th DLI) was
therefore placed at his disposal by Maj-Gen Graham.
At 0650 hours the next morning the battalion moved
from positions south-east of Bayeux, crossed the Seulles
and reached St-Léger. Here it met the Sherman tanks of
24th Lancers, with whom it was to co-operate in capturing
the Tessel–Bretteville Feature. At 0930 hours the joint
column set off for Point 103, crossing the rail line west
of le Bas d'Audrieu. Most of the DLI rode on the tanks,
although D Company – equipped with bicycles – had to
push these across country for much of the way.

After by-passing Audrieu, where fighting continued, the
column reached Point 103 at 1130 hours, 9 June. While
the infantry dismounted and formed up, their acting
CO, Major A.H. Dunn, went forward with the CO of
24th Lancers to survey the approaches to St-Pierre.

They were accompanied by Brigadier Cracroft and the CO of 147th Field Regiment, 8th Armoured Brigade's self-propelled artillery unit. Although little of St-Pierre was visible owing to the orchards and hedgerows surrounding it, they decided to attack the village frontally. To assist the advance, 147th Field Regiment's 25-pounders would fire a preliminary bombardment and lay a smoke screen from Point 103, while the Vickers machine guns of 2nd Cheshires' A Company provided indirect fire support. The assault would begin at 1730 hours, carried out by 8th DLI's C and D Companies, flanked to the east by C Squadron, 24th Lancers. Their specified limit of advance was the road from Tilly-sur-Seulles to Fontenay-le-Pesnel (now the D13). On reaching it they were to fire red and green flares, which would be the signal for A and B Companies to join them.

STAND D2: ST-PIERRE CHURCH

DIRECTIONS: Retrace your route to the D82 and continue south, passing the Château d'Audrieu (now a luxury hotel) on your left. About 1 km south of the château there is a road junction, next to which stands the water tower visible from Stand D1. If you want to visit Point 103, and can park safely, access is via a track that leads west towards the Ferme du Pont Roch.

Drive slowly along the D82 to St-Pierre. The views make the tactical significance of Point 103 immediately apparent. Just before you enter the village, look at the farm on your right (the Maison des Trois Cheminées on modern maps); this was 8th DLI's HQ during the battle for St-Pierre. Continue through the village to St-Pierre church (*below*). Park and walk through the churchyard to its western edge, overlooking the River Seulles.

THE ACTION: At 1745 hours, slightly later than intended, 8th DLI's C and D Companies advanced from Point 103. Initially, resistance was confined to indirect shell fire. However, on the outskirts of St-Pierre it was supplemented by machine guns and mortars, and

St-Pierre church, looking west. C Company, 8th DLI, occupied positions near here during the night of 9–10 June. *(Author)*

several members of Major John Leybourne's C Company were killed or wounded. B Company was therefore sent to reinforce the attack. Together with the leading companies, it pushed towards the main road. After heavy fighting, during which four of C Company's five officers became casualties (Leybourne among them), the objective was reached and the success signal sent up. Major Dunn then entered St-Pierre, establishing his HQ at the farm on its northern edge. Major C.L. Beattie's A Company took up positions on the north-west side of the village (Rue d'Audrieu), while Captain I.R. English's D Company dug in around the junction at the south-east corner (Stand D3). Major T.L.A. Clapton's B Company was about 500 metres behind D Company. Despite its heavy losses, C Company stayed near the church, in the positions which it had captured during the attack. Two 6-pounder troops (eight guns) from C Battery, 102nd Anti-Tank Regiment, RA, (Northumberland Hussars) also arrived, deploying their weapons around the village together with 8th DLI's anti-tank platoon (six guns) to cover likely approaches into St-Pierre. Having supported the attack, the 24th Lancers' C Squadron leaguered near Major Dunn's headquarters. The rest of the regiment remained on Point 103.

① 8th DLI battalion headquarters
② Site of Sherwood Rangers officers' deaths
   Base map: IGN 1512OT

le Haut
d'Audrieu

les Longs Champs

88

87

les Blochères

100

•POINT 103
(1944 Maps)

99

D82

92

les Bru

82

le Clos

76

78

St. épur

①

②

Maison
des Trois Cheminées

CRISTO

77

84

D4

le Long Bourg

R. Seulles

la Butte

Chemin
a Cour Péron

D 82

St-Pierre

82.5

D2

79

82

To
BAYEUX

D3

D13

Coop.
agric.

D13

53

76

FONTENA
LE-PESN

1,3 CT

Tilly-sur-Seulles

82

Éc.

Chapelle du Rosaire

D13

la Chapelle

les Chuchets

Motocross

52

79

To
JUVIGNY

0   0.5   1
Kilometres

An aerial view of St-Pierre and the Seulles floodplain (photo taken on 14 June).
(Keele University Air Photo Archive)

Key

a. Tilly-sur-Seulles

b. St-Pierre church (C Company,
   8th DLI, first position)

c. D Company, 8th DLI, first position

d. Road to Fontenay-le-Pesnel
   (modern D13)

e. Maisons des Trois Cheminées
   (8th DLI battalion headquarters)

f. Road to Point 103 (Rue d'Audrieu)

g. D Company second position

h. Road to Cristot (Rue de Cristot)

After a sleepless night, during which patrols established that the Seulles bridge was intact and in enemy hands, at 0615 hours on 10 June the British came under intense artillery and mortar fire. Almost immediately, infantry from 1st and 2nd Battalions of Panzer Lehr's 901st Panzergrenadier Regiment attacked, moving through the orchards and hedges around St-Pierre and closing in on the Durhams' positions. They were supported by several self-propelled guns, and possibly by elements of 12th SS Panzer Division (2. *Panzerkompanie*, with Panther tanks, plus part of the reconnaissance battalion), advancing from the south-east and east.

Outnumbered, tired and with only one officer, C Company's forward platoons were quickly overrun. A Company also came under pressure. Although most of its positions were held, some of its personnel withdrew towards battalion headquarters, where they were joined by a few survivors from C Company. Two of 8th DLI's anti-tank guns were lost (though later recovered), while those of the Northumberland Hussars were quickly limbered up and withdrawn. Meanwhile, panzers and infantry pushed into St-Pierre from the east, bringing B Company under close range fire and knocking out several of C Squadron's Shermans. Other elements of the squadron retreated to Point 103, taking their wounded commander, Major J. Noël Cowley, with them.

Following the initial shock, however, 8th DLI fought back determinedly. Every available man, among them the headquarters personnel, joined the defence of the farm on the northern edge of St-Pierre, around which most of the battalion had concentrated. Some of the Northumberland Hussars' gunners joined them, fighting as infantry. Tanks from 24th Lancers' A and B Squadrons also moved downhill from Point 103. Although the first of these was destroyed soon after entering the village, this at least had the effect of blocking the road to any further advance by the German armour. Partly as a result, by 1130 hours the German attack was halted. To prevent its resumption, the British smothered the surrounding

area with artillery fire. Some of this was provided by 147th Field Regiment, which had forward observers in St-Pierre (three of whom became casualties). However, much of the support came from the cruisers HMS *Orion* (eight 6-inch guns) and HMS *Argonaut* (ten 5.25-inch guns), which carried out numerous shoots, directed from the air, in the triangle Tilly–Juvigny–Fontenay-le-Pesnel. The RAF also played its part, sending fighter-bombers to attack the area south-east of St-Pierre. Under such overwhelming fire it proved impossible for the Panzer Lehr Division to resume its attack. Having withdrawn most of its personnel from the village, the 901st Panzergrenadier Regiment went back onto the defensive. Its attempt to re-capture St-Pierre had failed.

Anatol Petrov (a Latvian) was a corporal in the 7th Company of the Panzer Lehr Division's 901st Panzer-grenadier Regiment. This is his diary entry for 10 June.

'Early this morning we put in our attack. We had three self-propelled guns under command. We attacked a village. That was some show and some shooting. We shot up six tanks. Bullets were whistling overhead. As soon as we got beyond the village the artillery opened up, and I'll say there was confusion. Oh, that was certainly no fun. Nearly became a prisoner of war. Three of our vehicles gone... Then came a counter-attack by the English... They shot up several tanks and captured dozens of prisoners. After a long search we found

the vehicles but the enemy planes had found us and the artillery fire came down on us again. Some are wounded, L is killed. We proceed in short bounds to regimental headquarters and await further orders... At 10 p.m. Lehrmann came – contact with the company had been established. Eat our evening meal and await what may yet come. Shall I have to go forward again? Corporals G and K are missing. Thank God we are staying here overnight.'
Source: 50th Division Intelligence Summary, 20 June 1944.

Above: The view along the D13, looking east from D Company's first position. The entrance to the Rue de Cristot is on the left. A hundred metres along the D13, also on the left, are the grounds of a beautiful château, around which 18 and 16 Platoons were initially deployed. *(Author)*

STAND D3:
D COMPANY'S FIRST POSITION

DIRECTIONS: Leaving your vehicle at the church, turn left along the pavement beside the main road (D13) and walk uphill (east). Continue for 400 metres to the junction

shown in the photograph at the top of p.179. This is the position held by 8th DLI's D Company on the morning of 10 June.

THE ACTION: Unlike C and A Companies, Captain English's D Company was not exposed to the full force of the first German assault on 10 June. Nevertheless, by 0800 hours it was reporting tanks moving towards it along the road from Fontenay-le-Pesnel, and soon afterwards it was heavily attacked. Initial German efforts were concentrated against 17 Platoon, defending the junction between the Rue de Cristot and the D13. After suffering heavy casualties the platoon was forced to retreat. Aware that the flank of the rest of the company (which was slightly further east) was now exposed, Captain English ordered the other platoons to withdraw soon after. Fighting its way back to a position 300 metres to the north, the company regrouped around a farm on the north-east corner of St-Pierre. Here it linked up with B Company, deployed east of battalion HQ.

Captain (later Major) I.R. English, MC, recalled a detail of the fight for St-Pierre.

'In another part of the village Lieutenant [Peter] Laws [battalion intelligence officer], in spite of his wound, was moving from house to house, garden to garden – pausing for a few minutes to snipe at any German who showed himself. Then he moved on again. Laws was a good shot; taking careful aim and apparently oblivious of the noise of battle around him he picked off several of the enemy. [I] found him sniping most successfully from the top floor of a house. By this time Laws had propped himself up and was very weak from loss of blood. [I] had him evacuated immediately and for his gallantry during this morning of heavy fighting Laws was awarded the Military Cross.'

Source: P.J. Lewis & I.R. English, Into Battle with the Durhams: 8 D.L.I. in World War II, p. 249.

STAND D4:
D COMPANY'S HEADQUARTERS

DIRECTIONS: Walk north-east from Stand D3 along the Rue de Cristot, following the route of D Company's withdrawal. After ejecting D Company from its first position, three German tanks advanced up this road, driving a herd of terrified cattle before them. They were stopped by D Company's Lance-Sergeant S.P. Wallbanks, who fired three PIAT grenades, one of which bounced between the cows and under the leading tank's tracks! After about 500 metres, having passed the place where C Company's last officer, Captain J.N. Wheatley, was killed by a mortar bomb, you will reach the farm entrance shown overleaf. This was D Company's headquarters on 10–11 June.

THE ACTION: By the afternoon of 10 June the attackers' energies had diminished, and it was possible to re-organise 8th DLI. Most of the battalion remained concentrated at the northern end of the village (A/C Company in the orchards around battalion headquarters; D Company 200 metres to the south-east; and B Company in its first position astride the road to Cristot), although fighting patrols probed into St-Pierre as far as the church. The Northumberland Hussars' anti-tank guns were re-deployed, and two of the infantry's 6-pounders were recovered. Some of the wounded were evacuated, and at 2030 hours Lt-Col Lidwill, who had been 151st Brigade's acting CO since 7 June, returned and resumed command of the battalion. After dark a hot meal was supplied from Point 103, with highly beneficial effects on morale. During the evening 24th Lancers was also relieved by the Sherwood Rangers, which sent one squadron into St-Pierre to support the Durhams, while the rest of the regiment leaguered in the orchards just north-west of the village.

The night of 10–11 June was another restless one for the troops holding St-Pierre. Further counter-attacks were expected, and the village was shelled intermittently. The bombardment continued the following morning, with tragic consequences when the Sherwood Rangers' commander, his

Above: This is the entrance to the farm where D Company's headquarters was located on 10–11 June (Stand D4). The photo was taken from the eastern side of the Rue de Cristot, looking south. *(Author)*

Opposite: The junction between the Chemin du Haut de Sainte-Pierre and the Rue d'Audrieu, looking north. The plaque by the gate records the death of the acting CO of the Sherwood Rangers, Major M.H. Laycock, his adjutant (Captain Jones), and intelligence officer (Lt Head), all killed in the farmyard on the left. *(Author)*

adjutant and intelligence officer were killed, and the signal officer wounded by a single shell burst. Nevertheless, by midday the situation appeared stable enough for Lt-Col Lidwill to be able to attend a conference at 8th Armoured Brigade's headquarters on Point 103.

At 1620 hours the Durhams heard that 7th Armoured Division had reached Tilly, and briefly it seemed possible that a link-up might be established. However, barely had this information been received, and before Lidwill had returned, when St-Pierre was attacked again. This time the assault came from the east, in the shape of several Panzer IVs and Panthers, supported by infantry. Although the main aim of this attack seems to have been to cover a more serious thrust against Point 103, the Germans nevertheless penetrated to the northern edge of the village, enabling them to enfilade B Company's positions. Many casualties were suffered, among them the company commander, Major Clapton, who was mortally wounded. Major Dunn, who had led the battalion on 9–10 June, was also injured, as was the commander of the Northumberland Hussars' C Battery, Major G.R. Balfour. After one of their panzers had been destroyed and others damaged at short range by anti-tank rounds, however, the Germans withdrew. There were no further incidents overnight.

By 12 June events elsewhere on the battlefield had rendered the continued occupation of St-Pierre unnecessary. To conserve resources, it was decided to evacuate the village. Having suffered over 200 casualties in the battle

(among them five officers killed and at least six wounded), at 2315 hours the Durhams moved back to Point 103. From there, trucks took them to Cachy, 5 km south of Bayeux. In Captain English's words, 'Then everyone laid down and slept the sleep of the just.'

Reflecting the gallantry displayed by the defenders of St-Pierre, no fewer than 15 decorations were awarded after the battle. Of these, nine went to men of 8th DLI, and six to Northumberland Hussars. It seems highly unlikely that there were many other actions on a similar scale fought by the British during the Battle of Normandy that resulted in so many medals being awarded.

ENDING THE TOUR: From Stand D4 walk along the Chemin du Haut de Sainte-Pierre, which connects the eastern and western parts of St-Pierre. About half way along it, look left for a remarkable memorial to many of the British units that

Above: St-Pierre, as seen by the crews of the Panzer Lehr Division's tanks as they attacked late on 11 June. The Durhams' D Company was on the left, B Company was in the centre, and battalion headquarters was at the farm on the right. The road in the foreground is the Rue de Cristot. (Author)

The commemorative plaque to the Durham Light Infantry. *(Author)*

fought in this area. It takes the form of 72 grey slates (possibly more when you visit), attached to a stone wall. The crest and name of a regiment or division has been carved onto each. All of 50th Division's and 8th Armoured Brigade's combat units are commemorated here, together with other formations. There is a separate slate, inscribed with the crest and motto of the DLI, on the building's side wall.

Continue to the crossroads shown in the photo on p.183. As the memorial indicates, this is where the three Sherwood Rangers officers were killed on 11 June.

Turn left (south) at the crossroads and return to your vehicle along the Rue d'Audrieu. Be careful, since this road lacks pavements along part of its length.

From St-Pierre take the D13 to Tilly-sur-Seulles. This village was finally captured by British forces on 19 June. Although it opens only during the summer, the Museum of the Battle of Tilly is recommended. It is located in a beautiful 12th century chapel south-west of Tilly's main crossroads (see tour map). There is a memorial to 24th Lancers outside. There are several restaurants and shops in Tilly.

To visit the graves of many of the soldiers who died in this area continue west on the D13 for 1 km to the Tilly-sur-Seulles Commonwealth War Graves Commission (CWGC) cemetery. Here you will find the final resting place of the Sherwood Rangers officers killed on 11 June (Block II, J1, 2 and 3), as well as the grave of Captain Keith Douglas (also of the Sherwood Rangers), Britain's finest Second World War poet, killed at Point 103 two days earlier (Block I, E2). Others who died near here are buried in the CWGC cemetery near Hottot-les-Bagues. To find this cemetery, drive south

MUSEUM OF THE BATTLE OF TILLY

Musée de la Bataille de Tilly, Chapelle Notre Dame du Val, 14250 Tilly-sur-Seulles; tel: +33 (0)6 07 59 46 02; web: <www.museetilly.free.fr> Open May–Sept, closed Oct–Apr. Opening during the closed season is possible by arrangment with the curator, Stéphane Jacquet, on the number above. Entrance fee.

for about 1½ km along the D6 from Tilly until you reach the T-junction with the D9. Turn right and the cemetery is 750 metres along the road, on the right hand side.

Alternatively, to visit Bayeux, head north from Tilly along the D6 for 13 km. You may wish to stop *en route* at the Jérusalem CWGC cemetery, which is on the right 100 metres beyond the right hand turn (D187) to Chouain. This is the smallest British war cemetery in France, with 46 British graves, and one Czech. Most of them are from the DLI, including two padres and Private Jack Banks, 16 years old when he was killed on 21 July 1944.

PART FOUR
ON YOUR RETURN

FURTHER RESEARCH

Following your return from Normandy, or perhaps even before you go, you may want to find out more about the events described in this book.

One way to begin is to use the internet, typing such terms as 'Gold Beach Normandy' into a search engine. However, although you may discover some very good sites, others are much less impressive, or even misleading. Nevertheless, the rapidly evolving nature of the internet makes it worth consideration, especially when seeking out specialised information (for example on the Atlantic Wall defences), or to identify archive contact details and to order books.

Much of the research for this work was carried out using the original war diaries of the units concerned, which are held at the *UK National Archives* (formerly the Public Record Office) in south-west London. Access is possible to members of the general public on application for a reader's ticket. The majority of the records come from class WO 171, which contains the war diaries of most British units involved in the north-west European campaign. Classes DEFE 2 (Combined Operations), WO 208 (Military Intelligence Directorate) and CAB 44 (battle narratives and analyses) also include many relevant papers, as do at least a dozen other record groups. Other material, notably some important German documents, was gathered during a research trip to the *US National Archives* in Washington DC. The *Imperial War Museum* (IWM) holds extensive written records and photographs, as well as cine film and recorded interviews with veterans. The *D-Day Museum* in Southsea, near Portsmouth, plus a range of excellent regimental and corps

Page 186: British soldiers inspect WN-35's 50-mm gun emplacement. Despite damage to the seaward side, where the steel reinforcing rods have been thrown upward by direct hits, the gun was captured intact. *(IWM B5252)*

Below. The price. The grave of Major H.V. Duke, 2nd Devons' C Company commander, killed at le Hamel on D-Day. *(Author)*

USEFUL ADDRESSES

UK National Archives, Public Record Office, Kew, Richmond, Surrey TW9 4DU; tel: 020 8876 3444; web: <www.nationalarchives.gov.uk>.

US National Archives, The National Archives and Records Administration, 8601 Adelphi Road, College Park, Maryland MD 20740-6001; tel: +01 866 272 6272; web: <www.archives.gov>.

Imperial War Museum, Lambeth Road, London SE1 6HZ; tel: 020 7416 5320; email: <mail@iwm.org.uk>; web: <www.iwm.org.uk>.

D–Day Museum and Overlord Embroidery, Clarence Esplanade, Southsea PO5 3NT; tel: 023 9282 7261; web: <www.ddaymuseum.co.uk>.

British Library, 96 Euston Road, London NW1 2DB; tel: 0843 208 1144; <email: reader-services-enquiries@bl.uk>; web: <www.bl.uk>.

The Aerial Reconnaissance Archives (TARA) [formerly University of Keele Air Photo Library], The National Collection of Aerial Photography, RCAHMS, John Sinclair House, 16 Bernard Terrace, Edinburgh, EH8 9NX; tel: 0131 662 1456; web: <http://aerial.rcahms.gov.uk>.

Library and Archives Canada, 395 Wellington Street, Ottawa, Ontario K1A 0N3; tel: +01 866 578 7777; web: <www.collectionscanada.gc.cal>.

museums dotted around the country are also worth visiting, if you have the opportunity. The contemporary maps used in the 'Battle Zone Normandy' series came mainly from the *British Library* in central London.

Among other sources consulted were the regimental histories of 50th Division's units, plus personal memoirs and some German divisional histories. These vary enormously in quality, and many are long out of print. The easiest way to gain access is probably to use your local inter-library loan service. Alternatively, you can try contacting the IWM or the regimental museum of the unit concerned. A comprehensive list of British regimental museums (with contact details) can be found on the internet at <www.armymuseums.org.uk>.

Some useful secondary sources include:

Normandy, D-Day: With the Green Howards of the 50th Division, The Green Howards Regimental Museum, Richmond, 1997.

Bernage, Georges, *Gold, Juno, Sword*, Editions Heimdal, Bayeux, 2003.

Chazette, Alain, *Le Mur de L'Atlantique en Normandie*, Editions Heimdal, Bayeux, 2000.

Clay, Ewart W., *The Path of the 50th: The Story of the 50th*

(Northumbrian) Division in the Second World War, Gale & Polden, Aldershot, 1950.

D'Este, Carlo, *Decision in Normandy: The Unwritten Story of Montgomery and the Allied Campaign*, Collins, London, 1983.

Dunphie, Christopher, & Johnson, Garry, *Gold Beach: Inland from King – June 1944*, Leo Cooper/Pen & Sword Books, Barnsley, 1999.

Ellis, L.F., *Victory in the West: Volume I – The Battle of Normandy*, HMSO, London, 1962.

Forfar, John, *From Omaha to the Scheldt – The Story of 47 Royal Marine Commando*, Tuckwell Press, East Linton, 2001.

Harrison, Gordon A., *United States Army in World War II: The European Theatre of Operations – Cross-Channel Attack*, US Army, Washington DC, 1951.

Hart, Russell A., *Clash of Arms: How the Allies Won in Normandy*, Lynne Rienner Publishers, London, 2001.

Isby, David C. (ed.), *Fighting the Invasion: The German Army at D-Day*, Greenhill Books, London, 2000.

Isby, David C. (ed.), *Fighting in Normandy: The German Army from D-Day to Villers-Bocage*, Greenhill Books, London, 2001.

Lewis, P.J., & English, I.R., *Into Battle with the Durhams: 8 D.L.I. in World War II*, London Stamp Exchange, London, 1990.

Meyer, Hubert, *The History of the 12. SS Panzerdivision 'Hitlerjugend'*, J.J. Fedorowicz Publishing, Winnipeg, 1994.

Miller, Russell, *Nothing less than Victory: the Oral History of D-Day*, Michael Joseph, London, 1993.

Pitcairn-Jones, L.J., *Operation 'Neptune': The Landings in Normandy, 6th June 1944*, HMSO, London, 1994 edition.

Saunders, Tim, *Gold Beach – Jig: Jig Sector and West – June 1944*, Leo Cooper/Pen & Sword Books, Barnsley, 2002.

Synge, W.A.T., *The Story of the Green Howards, The Green Howards Regimental Museum*, Richmond, 1952.

Zetterling, Niklas, *Normandy 1944: German Military Organization, Combat Power and Organizational Effectiveness*, J.J. Fedorowicz Publishing, Winnipeg, 2000.

INDEX